Revolution
in the
Garden

MEMOIRS OF THE GARDENKEEPER

MORE PRAISE FOR *REVOLUTION IN THE GARDEN*

"Dell Williams' memoir reads like a study in the sixties revolution and its long term effects on twentieth-century American women. Feminism happens everywhere, but only in America did we take off our pants and consciously liberate our sexuality within communal sisterhood. The historical knowledge Dell transmits to us through this book is alive with passion. Blessed be this foremother of the sexual revolution!" —VICKI NOBLE

"I read this wonderful memoir in one sitting. It reminded me of what courage and initiative it took to start 'Eve's Garden' and how the sisterhood of the 70s was all about empowering ourselves and each other to make the world a better place for women. We must keep that message alive." —LEONORE TIEFER, Ph.D.

"Dell Williams' revealing memoir is a revelation about her life and her pioneering contribution to the enhancement of women's sexuality. Because of her work, and the other women's sexuality boutiques that followed, information and sex is sager and more exuberant than it might have been." —REBECCA CHALKER

"Dell Williams has gone through life with the innocence of a Forrest Gump, walking into the eye of the storm. The quest for a sexually healthy society put her mentor, Wilhelm Reich, in the grave; as a pioneer of the Women's Movement, Dell held on to the torch. Her biography recounts the kind of sexual rites and wrongs that are all too familiar to most people. In the sex field, too often polarized by 'Martians' and Puritans, Dell has had her own steadfast agenda— to help men and women relate in the most intimate way."

—EDWARD EICHEL

Revolution
in the
Garden

MEMOIRS OF THE GARDENKEEPER

Dell Williams
FOUNDER OF EVE'S GARDEN

AND Lynn Vannucci

Revolution in the Garden: Memoirs of the Gardenkeeper
by Dell Williams and Lynn Vannucci
© Silverback Books, Inc.

Published by Silverback Books

Book Design: Future Studio Los Angeles

ISBN 1-59637-038-6

Printed and bound in Hong Kong

SILVERBACK
BOOKS INC.

Dedication

It has long been my unassailable belief that orgasmic women can change the world. By this I mean that a woman who is unfettered sexually is unfettered politically, socially, and economically, and she is unstoppable. I dedicate this book to all of us who are in the process of rediscovering our sexual, essential, unstoppable selves.

This book is also dedicated to my beloved brother, Lorenz Zetlin, who stood with me at my kitchen table to send out the first orders for Eve's Garden. He will be greatly missed.

DELL WILLIAMS,
The Gardenkeeper

Contents

Acknowledgments

The authors would like to thank all of the women and men who gave of their time so generously and agreed to be interviewed for this book: Deb Anapol, Jacqui Ceballos, Rebecca Chalker, Ani Colt, Marcia Corbett, Alan DeValle, Betty Dodson, Edward Eichel, Riane Eisler, Eve Ensler, Melinda Gallagher, Sally Miller Gearhart, Hanny Lightfoot-Klein, Marty Klein, Emily Kramer, Alice Ladas, Brenda Marston, Stephanie Moro, Gina Ogden, Carol Queen, Linda Savage, Annie Sprinkle, Gloria Steinem, Regena Thomashauer, and Janet Wolfe.

The authors would also like to thank Howard Cohl, Amy Goldsmith, and John Mehr for support, direction, and unfailing good humor in the course of writing this book. We would also like to thank the editors, especially John Sollami and Susie Yates, for accurate, timely, and wise editorial contributions.

Dell expresses her thanks as follows: "First, to Betty Dodson, whose courageous stand as an advocate for masturbation and women's sexual liberation inspired me in 1974 to create Eve's Garden. I also want to acknowledge Lonnie Barbach, Ruth Westheimer, Barbara Bartlett, Judy Kuriansky, Alice Ladas, Dolores Keller, Gina Ogden, Ziva Quitney, Helen Colton, Janet Wolfe, Robert Birch, Norman Sherzer, Bryce Britton, Annie Sprinkle, and Cosi Fabian—as well as all the other therapists, counselors, and sex educators who looked upon Eve's Garden as an educational resource for their clients. Thanks to the college professors who included Eve's Garden as part of their Human Sexuality courses, and to *Ms. Magazine,* Barnard College's *Barnard Bulletin,* and all the feminist and lesbian publications that published our ads and our story when we were too controversial for the general press; I especially thank Louise Bernikow, who wrote the first story ever about Eve's Garden. Thank you to David Ramsdale, Dr.

Alexander Lowen, Michael Scollaro, Peggy Grasso, Alan Lowen, Lucille Bella, Jacqueline Bishop, Jacqui Ceballos, Selma Rosen, Judith Kravitz, the Reverend Diane Berke, my Bliss Sisters, Ani Colt, Suzann Robins, Bettye Lane, and Elissa K. West, who influenced my wholeness and spiritual well-being. Thank you to all of the women, past and present, who shared their passion and dedication to the goals of Eve's Garden—our store managers Suzanne Erick, Ninia Baehr, Marcia Corbett, Lorraine Melendez, and Kim Ibricevic, and our staff Ruth Libby, Patty Welch-Hall, Gina Georgaras, Samantha Armor, Elissa Domroe, Rainbow Reitz, Pam Weems, Mara Gottleib, Coleen Davenport, Peggy McDonald, Yolanda DeJesus, Rosa Quiles, Ida Ibricevic, Tara Visdervio, Florence Ragusa, and Sultana Pashalides. Thank you to Pat Snibbe, who designed our first catalog, as well as to Bunne Hartman and Durga Bernhard for their powerful logo images; Linda Karen Bisgaard and Lynette Brannon, who contributed their woman-empowering poetry; and to The Women's Press Collective, who always met our printing deadlines with patience and fortitude. And last I would like to thank the brave women who are our customers and continue to be willing to take a step outside their comfort zone to reclaim, affirm, and celebrate their powerful sexual–spiritual heritage."

Lynn would like to thank Shane Adler, Jeffrey Barker, Bob Bravard, Gloria Briggs, Sally Brightcloud, Linda Butterfield, Mary Coploff, Nancy Ellis-Bell, Sal Glynn, Michelle Guyette, Jackie and Jim Harvey, Karen Harvey, Bob Hoffmann, Anne Kilkenny and the Bookstore Babes, Rita Lakin, Leslie Linnebur, Christy Litchfield, Lynn Lytle, Virginia Martin, Jack Neal, Sheila Smith Neal, Pan, Beth Press, Kris Radish, Ruth Sander, Carol and Paul Schofield, Ginny Seay, James Simpkins, Sally Smith, Stephen Smith, Leeya Thompson, Philip Vannucci, Stacey Vannucci, and, most very especially, her sister, Fifi Gallagher.

Part One

Learning

Chapter One

1922

Women didn't have orgasms.

Not officially.

Not in 1922, the year that I was born.

In 1922, Isadora Duncan was dancing, Bessie Smith was singing, Georgia O'Keefe was painting, Harry Houdini was escaping, and Gertrude Stein, F. Scott Fitzgerald, and James Joyce were writing—this was the year that *Ulysses* was finally published, after nearly a decade of censorship battles, and all 500 copies that were shipped to the United States were seized by government authorities, and burned.

This was the year that Mussolini marched on Rome and formed the Fascist government, that the Union of Soviet Socialist Republics was created, and that a reparations commission fixed Germany's compensation for material losses and suffering caused by the Great War at 132 billion gold marks, triggering the beginnings of German inflation and setting the stage for World War II.

In 1922, King Tut's tomb was unearthed from the Valley of Kings, insulin was isolated and used for the first time in the treatment of diabetes, and it had been two years since the 19th amendment was ratified.

Women had the vote but we still didn't have orgasms.

Women had "hysterical crises."

"What is a hysterical crisis? On the clinical level, excitomotor paroxysmic accidents accompanied by convulsions and crises of inhibition with loss of consciousness, lethargy, or catalepsy . . ..["1]

Hysterical crises were *accidents*, and they were also the prescribed relief for a disorder characterized by a set of symptoms "including but not limited to fainting (syncope), edema or hyperemia (congestion caused by fluid retention, either localized or general), nervousness, insomnia, sensations of heaviness in the abdomen, muscle spasms, shortness of breath, loss of appetite for food or for sex with the approved male partner, and sometimes a tendency to cause trouble for others, particularly members of the patient's immediate family."[2]

Thwarted feminine desire turned us into busybodies (and worse), but our desire itself was the disease, and it was treated medically.

Finding a husband was the first course of treatment recommended for virgins who presented with symptoms of "hysteria." Doctors generated handsome incomes for themselves by performing in-office genital massage to relieve the suffering of married women, widows, and nuns. "Heroic" measures such as clitoridectomies were used to cure the most difficult cases of "hysteria"—*nymphomania* and *chronic masturbation*.

I am not referring here to some chronologically or geographically distant culture passing off the barbaric practice of female genital mutilation as a societal norm, or prettifying it by calling it circumcision. I am not referring to some of the darker and more salacious practices of medieval "medicine." I am talking about how female desire has been dealt with in "modern" Western medical tradition, in our own country, in the long, civilized century into which all of you who are able right now to read these words were born: women's sexual desire was officially categorized by the American

---

[1] Maines, Rachel P., *The Technology of Orgasm.*
[2] Ibid.

Psychiatric Association as a medical condition until 1952.

But it's not my intention here to delve into the details of how female sexual desire has been perverted by established patriarchal authority for the past 5,000 years or so. Rachel P. Maines has already done that in her scholarly and provocative book, *The Technology of Orgasm.*

What I want to do is to address what's happened in the fifty or so years since the women of America have been officially allowed to get good and horny without the threat of being subjected to corrective surgery—how far we have come and how, so far, some very basic concepts remain frustratingly just outside the reach of a collective emotional and imaginative and, importantly, political ability to digest them.

I want to clear up some misconceptions about the women's movement of the 1960s and 1970s, of which I am a proud veteran. I want to cheer the young women out there today who, in spite of the failures of a forty-year-old "sexual revolution" and what is benignly called a "conservative backlash" in the mainstream media, are still bringing fresh energy and ideas to the fight for women's rights. I want to rail a little bit about how, in these early years of a brand new century, women's sexual desire is still being classified as a disorder, albeit in new ways—how the big pharmaceutical companies are currently in hot competition with each other for the billion-dollar bonanza that awaits the first one of them to come up with a chemical cure that will fix us once and for all. I want to recommend a few books that I believe are essential reading, books that will shock and outrage and educate their reader, and move her to a better understanding of her body, her power, and herstory.

And, along the way, I want to tell you the story of how a nice Jewish girl from the Bronx ended up owning a sex toy store.

Chapter Two

The Power
of Naming Things

In 1974 I founded the first woman-owned and -operated sexuality boutique and mail order service in America. My store was designed expressly to serve women in discovering and embracing their own sexual power. I was fifty-two years old then, a successful advertising executive, and an activist in the women's rights movement. I sat one day at my desk at the advertising agency where I was working, casting about for a name for my new venture, when the poster over my desk caught my eye.

The poster was created for the National Organization for Women's (NOW) first Women's Sexuality Conference, an event I had helped organize in June of 1973. The illustration on the poster had been drawn by a friend of mine, Betty Dodson. It was a reworking of Leonardo da Vinci's Vitruvian Man—a woman in a circle, naked and outstretched, muscled and full of the sort of energy that made one expect motion, open-eyed and open-armed. "Like Eve," I thought, emerging with awe and fearlessness into her wonderful, unknown world, before she was shamed into that fig-leaf getup.

Let me give you a little herstory lesson.

The Old Testament is the record of a holy political war—the conquest and massacre of settled, agricultural, Neolithic civilizations by the nomadic pastoralist tribes. Like everyone else in the Near East, the settled people of the Old Testament lived in matriarchal societies, and they practiced Goddess worship. The nomadic tribes invaded the fertile lands of the settled peoples after their ecologically devastating mode of animal husbandry had depleted their own stomping grounds. They were intent on instituting their system of patrilineal property and inheritance rights. In order to assure the establishment of economic policies that favored the patriarchal tribes, the Moon Mother Astarte had to be replaced by the tribes' Sky-and-Thunder God. The Canaanite women who practiced their sensual, joyful moon rites were slaughtered, and their ancient, earth-based religion was demonized. The sacred symbols of the Mother Goddess—the moon and the serpent and the fig tree, which previously had been associated with woman-wisdom—were made into dark, evil icons. The Great Mother's oral mythology was stolen, recast, and written down by male prophets and thus given textual authority as "the word of God."[3]

The Serpent Goddess, Great Mother, Creatrix of the Universe, had been remythed[4] into an afterthought, some guy's rib, both gullible and malignant enough to be duped by a snake and get humanity tossed out of paradise.

Eve had been scapegoated.

Since the time of the Old Testament, it has been a matter of

---

[3] Primary resources for this woefully abbreviated herstory are two magnificent books: *The Great Cosmic Mother*, by Monica Sjoo and Barbara Mor, and *When God Was a Woman*, by Merlin Stone; get them; read them; revel in the archaeological and anthropological facts they contain.

[4] For a full discussion on remything, and so much more, please read Riane Eisler's beautiful book, *Sacred Pleasure*.

policy that woman is inherently defective. Our nature is base, our minds are weak, our bodies are shameful. Is it any wonder that our sense of ourselves is diminished, or that so many of us have conformed so contritely to male models of social and economic and political structure, to say nothing of the male model of sexual pleasure?

How efficient debasement is when you want to keep a group of people unstable, unsure, in line!

"Eve," I thought that day at my desk, "I'm going to help you reclaim your garden. And I'm going to invite every other woman I can possibly reach to come back home into paradise with you."

> *Eve's Garden is created to empower women to celebrate their sexuality as a positive, nourishing, and creative force in their lives.*
>
> *An outgrowth of the Women's Rights Movement, Eve's Garden seeks to erase the sense of shame and guilt experienced by countless women as a result of a society that historically condemns the sexual nature of women as sinful.*
>
> *Our version of "Eve" is a transformation from a fallen, shamed woman to a strong, powerful woman proud of her strength, sensitivity, and sexuality.*
>
> *To that purpose we have created a comfortable, elegant, and educational environment for women to explore the tools of pleasure, the books, and other enlightening materials to enhance mind, body, and spirit.*
>
> *We seek to encourage women to take responsibility for their own sexuality, honor the sacredness of*

sex, and clearly understand that bodily pleasure and spiritual joy are one, and an inalienable right.

This is an excerpt from our original mission statement, in 1974, the first year that Eve's Garden was in business. It's a powerful statement, no less radical now than when I wrote it, and it still serves as inspiration for me and for the people who work with me at Eve's Garden. It still hits the mark.

But, myself, I started out wide of the mark.

I'm 82 years old now. It's no secret that lifelong curiosity and willingness to learn can keep your mind and spirit, and even to some extent your body, youthful. I was fortunate to be born with a restless intellect and rather insatiable appetites because, from where I started out, I had a long way to travel to the garden.

Chapter Three

A Seedling
in Rocky Soil

Roughly two million Russian and Eastern European Jews emigrated to America between 1880 and 1914, fleeing mounting religious persecution and economic restrictions in their homelands, a population movement second only to the one caused by the Irish famine in the mid-nineteenth century as the greatest migration of modern times. My parents were among them.

You might choose to read any one of the marvelous and wrenching accounts of life for the new American immigrant that are offered for sale at New York's Lower East Side Tenement Museum— Rose Cohen's *Out of the Shadow* is one of the most moving—to gain a perspective on a typical journey to the New World. My parents, however, did not come in steerage. My father's people had been successful in the Russian theater, and my mother's had owned a thriving general store in Lipkany, in what is now Moldova. My parents were refugees with a little bit more than the usual financial and educational wherewithal.

My father, who spoke three languages, French among them, fled to Paris as a young man and set himself up as a dress designer. My mother, the youngest of six children, left Lipkany at fifteen with her sister, Dora, to live with their brother, Simon; Simon had emigrated a few years earlier and was writing for a socialist newspaper in Paris, and there my parents met.

In 1914, when Mom was eighteen and Dad was twenty-five and in danger of being conscripted into the French army, they sailed in a stateroom of an ocean liner to New York Harbor. They married and set up housekeeping in the Bronx. Dad went to work designing women's clothing for a firm that sold to Bendel's and Bergdorf Goodman's. Dad was also an obsessive athlete—bicycle racing and speed skating and tennis. He taught my mother how to play tennis, and she became passionate about the game.

Most of the stories of my first years are lost to me—lost among the demands of my father's career and his compulsion to play sports, and my mother's whirlwind life of tennis dates and tournaments—but there is one story I do know: I died when I was three years old.

I was very sick for several days, and on the third day three doctors told my mother that I had died. Two of the doctors left my bedroom after they delivered the news of my demise to her, and the third one stayed on with Mom. He was waiting for a nurse to come to take me from my deathbed, waiting to see if he would have to sedate my mother after I had been removed from her, waiting, in immaculate, airless silence, for my mother to understand her own grief and surrender to it. And then my mother heard a noise, and it was me, making noise and moving. In spite of what the doctors had said, there I was, alive anyway.

My mother used to tell me that story with awe, beyond tears.

I like to think of it as the first time I defied established authority.

My father's name was Isaac Zetlin. He immigrated to France from

Minsk. My mother was born Sarah Bronstein. My own birth certificate, from Lying-In Hospital in Manhattan, read, simply, "August 5, 1922, Female" for many days after I was born.

There are several stories about how I got my name. Sometimes my mother would tell me I was named for Floyd Dell, the writer who was one of the founders of the radical journal *The Masses*, an early supporter of birth control education and Margaret Sanger's efforts toward it, and a part of the coterie of men around John Reed, the American journalist best known for his book, *Ten Days That Shook the World*. Mom read one of Dell's stories while she was in the hospital having me, and the story impressed her. She decided then that I would be *Dell* too.

Other times she told me that I was named for her sister. It is a Jewish custom to name a new baby for someone who has died. My mother's sister, Hindel, had passed away, and, at times, I was told that my name was derived in honor of her.

Once in a while Mom would tell me she chose my name because there were very few *Dell*'s in the world and she wanted to give me a name that would be unique. I always liked this story the most. Though I'm sure it was a combination of all three scenarios that led my parents to settle on a name for their firstborn, I liked best the idea that my mother, who was a creative woman, wanted me to have a name for which there were few models, so I'd have to make my own identity out of it.

When my brother was born three and a half years later, he got an interesting name too: *Lorenz*.

Lorenz Zetlin. Dell Zetlin. Pretty unique.

My mother was a tiny woman, like me, no more than 5′2″. She was quite fashionable—my father probably designed most of her clothes—and we had a fashionable home too. Panels of red and gray velvet hung from the walls—a shockingly avant-garde form of interior design at the time—and we had a grand piano in the living room.

We listened to Caruso records on our Victrola, and my father sang in the chorus of an opera company. My parents went out to the opera together every chance they got. They went out to concerts, and out to the theater, and out to smart restaurants, although the only times I remember them entertaining were on my birthday, and my brother's.

Lorenz and I each got a party, every year, and they were big treats with lots of friends and sweets and games and a big cake to celebrate us, but no presents. The parties took place in Crotona Park, just across the street from where we lived (Mom was smart about not wanting a lot of sticky-fingered little kids invading her well-decorated rooms). They were purposefully impromptu affairs that left the invitees with no time to shop for the birthday girl or boy; a few of our little friends were from families that weren't as well-to-do as our own, and Mom didn't want to make the parents of those kids feel burdened by the obligation of a gift.

While, as an adult, I have grown to appreciate, and to admire, Mom's intent in providing a party that didn't require the price of a gift for admission, at the time I was most troubled and confused by my lack of a big pile of birthday presents: other kids' birthday parties seemed to me to always center around the ritual of gift opening. I remember thinking that Lorenz and I weren't as well-liked or deserving or some such thing as other boys and girls.

My father had left the design firm where he was employed and, with a partner, started his own dress manufacturing company where he was the solo design talent. He was a member of a great many sports teams and was off every summer evening to bicycle, and every winter evening to skate. My mother was having her share of athletic triumphs too. She competed in New York City's annual city-park tournament and won the women's singles championship for seven consecutive years, from 1920 until 1927.

In fact, Mom was such a good tennis player, as well as so chicly dressed for the sport, that her partners began referring to her as "our Suzanne," after Suzanne Lenglen. Suzanne Lenglen was a French woman who won six Wimbledon titles between 1919 and 1926, and she was responsible for adopting as her tennis uniform the sleeveless blouses and shorter skirts still fashionable today on the courts. The nickname stuck to Mom—even Dad started to call her "Suzanne," and the silver cups I still have on my shelves are engraved not to Sarah, but to "Susan Zetlin."

In 1927 my mother decided that she would give up the title of City Champion to a younger player—to pass the torch, so to speak—and then she always regretted that she threw the match that last year because Mayor Jimmy Walker himself presented the first place trophy to the winner.

One of the other things Mom did during these years was arrange for the integration of the tennis courts at the city's public parks where mixed doubles—matches that mixed men and women players—had never been allowed. Mom did this by challenging the best male player in her club to a match, with the creation of a mixed doubles category as the stake.

Mom won the match.

Her victory predated Billie Jean King's over Bobby Riggs by fifty years.

My mother was a woman of strength, albeit one who was taxed to the very limits of her personal fortitude. She came from a long line of strong women and therefore gained this virtue quite honestly. My grandmother, Mom's mom, was known by the townsfolk in Lipkany as a *balabuste*—from the Yiddish *baalit Habayit*. (*Baalit Habayit* means "owner of the home," though I urge you to pronounce the word *balabuste* out loud right now; I'm no student of linguistics, but I can make a guess about where a certain slang expression for a strong woman comes from.)

Anyway, back to Mom.

In order to have the free time that she needed to play in her tennis matches, Mom had to arrange for childcare for my brother and me. The arrangement she made was ingenious for the time. Though Mom always had what was referred to then as "colored help," it hit her that other young mothers in our neighborhood were probably lacking adequate time to pursue their own interests too, so she went to see a man who owned one of the empty storefronts in our neighborhood, rented it from him, and turned it into a sort of playroom for all of us kids. Our mothers took turns coming there to watch over us. I think it was probably the first day care center in the Bronx.

I don't think my mother started the childcare center from any political motivation—this was the 1920s; no one was talking about the inherent value of women's work or how the hard work that women did, cooking, cleaning, grocery shopping, and raising children, contributed to their own family's standard of living, let alone the national economy—and they certainly weren't concerned about the low wages that were paid to the already overburdened "colored help." Mom just did it because she saw how she and the other women around her—all the other young mothers and their helpers— were impeded from both fulfilling their obligations to their families and satisfying their own need for leisure activity. She saw a way to make life a little easier for all of them, and she acted on it.

❧

Most of my memories are from after "the Crash."

My father lost his dress manufacturing company, and he never did get back into design after that. He still worked in the garment industry, sporadically, as a sewing machine operator. My mother was forced to give up her life of luxury and go to work. She made from ten to fifteen dollars a week working as a dress finisher. Still, the rent on our Crotona Park place was too high, so we moved to a smaller apartment on Gun Hill Road. We became poor when I was at an impressionable age, seven, and we stayed really poor until I was nearly seventeen.

My father seemed to think of the Depression as a personal vacation. He spent most of it on a bike or in a pair of skates. He also let my mother know that it had never really been his idea to have us kids; so, on top of losing her life of leisure and having to go out to work, Mom found herself with two kids who were completely dependent on her for their support.

It was a struggle for Mom. She didn't have anyone any longer to help take care of my brother and me, and I ended up being a little mommy for my brother while my mother was at work all day.

We were dispossessed three times. No matter that I now know it is no shame to be poor, or that being poor was certainly not uncommon during the Depression, the memory of coming home from school and seeing all of our furniture out on the street can still make my eyes well up with tears of anger and humiliation.

After our third dispossession, Mom and Dad separated for a time. Actually, what happened was that my father left one day and, except for a single, short, surprise visit to Lorenz and me one afternoon in our schoolyard, he didn't show up again in our lives for nearly five years. My brother and I frequently went to court with Mom to claim the ten dollars a week Dad was supposed to pay her in child support.

Mom and Lorenz and I ended up living for long stretches of time in furnished rooms, first in the house of a grumpy, scary old man, and then with an old lady named Mrs. Moses. I remember that one Thanksgiving Day while we were at Mrs. Moses's, Mom cooked us a fairly meager holiday dinner and we ate it from atop a trunk because we had no dining table.

Those years of living in furnished rooms and being dragged off to court became even harder for me as I grew into a preteen and a teenager. My brother and I never invited our friends to our homes, so ashamed were we of our drab headquarters.

It was a rocky way to live, but I got used to it. Kids can get used to a lot of things, especially when they don't know how different things could be, and, anyway, this was at a time when a lot of little kids were more independent than they are today. A lot of kids were left alone during the Depression while their parents worked at any job they could get, and childhood itself wasn't as protected or sentimental a thing as it has become in the decades since. Paradoxically, the streets back then were safer places for kids to be.

But my mother, I don't think, ever got over her resentment of the way we had to live. As a kid, before the Crash, I have memories of her being able to make me laugh, of being really bright and light on her feet. After the Crash, she just sort of lost her spark, her sense of humor. Even I could see, even at just eight and nine years old, how very difficult it was for her, and I grew up wanting to do something for her to make her feel a little happier, a little better.

As I organized decades' worth of personal memorabilia in order to write this book, I came across one particular photograph of my mother during this period, and, in this photograph, she is smiling. Perhaps it will give you an idea of how very much her spirit abandoned her when I tell you that I was surprised such a photograph existed: I have no memory of my mother cracking a smile, not even one, after Black Friday plunged the country into the Great Depression.

Helping other people was a thing that made my mother feel better and that would, even after the Crash, animate her. She organized for the union in her factory; she was the chairperson of her women's garment worker's group. I think of this union work of hers as an extension of the way she had earlier handled day care for Lorenz and me: she saw a little problem and solved it in her own little community.

All big movements start in the smaller community.[5]

I came to see, as I grew up, that my mother's involvement with her union, and in her little community, was probably what shaped my own liberal views. My mother may not have been able to verbalize to me—or may not have really even known it herself—that she believed our society had to become more responsive and supportive of the needs of its members, especially its women, but she showed it to me through the work that she did in her life, and I'm so grateful to her for it.

I also often think that the fierceness of my commitment to

---

[5] My mother was a huge fan of Eleanor Roosevelt.

the women's movement came out of wanting to somehow make up for the powerlessness Mom suffered during that time: I'm 82, and my mother died over a quarter of a century ago. Yet I still sometimes think of myself as that little girl trying to give her mother something to smile about.

I should also say that, while my family was impoverished, our life was in many ways still fairly genteel. My parents valued art. There was always music in our house—Mozart, Beethoven, and Liszt are still among my favorites. Mother took us to art museums—the Metropolitan, of course, where I could spend an entire day lost in wonder, and the Museum of Natural History, which was my brother's favorite outing—though I wonder if we would or could have gone as often as we did if the admission to those museums hadn't been free.

My father became utterly devoted, at this time, to improving his singing voice. I remember, during the latter part of the Depression, when he finally came back home, that he'd sit at our piano—which, incredibly, made all of our various moves with us—and practice singing. Or, rather, what he practiced was scales, and the repetition used to drive the rest of us mad. He painted, too, during this period, in oils; tremendous, large canvases. He did one of the sacrifice of Abraham, which my brother still has, and he painted a portrait of me.

My father was emotionally remote. I still feel the distance he kept from me and my brother and our mother as more impoverishing than our economic circumstances. His remoteness has left a gap in me I feel even now; to this day, whenever I see a little girl holding her father's hand or riding up on his shoulders, I am overcome by how tender a father and daughter bond can be. I know, because I have heard many of my own friends speak of their fathers in these terms, that it can be a relationship that can be cherished and empowering for a young girl. I don't know how a person can miss something she never had, but I feel that because of Dad's coldness I missed out on something that could have been extraordinary.

I also know that painting my portrait was a way for my father to show his love for me, which was perhaps the only way he knew how.

One thing that could still make my mother really happy, even after the Crash, was to go out to the opera. Dad took her as often as he could. Even when he couldn't afford seats he frequently managed the few dollars for standing room. He and Mom would get all dressed up in their best clothes and go off and stand together through an entire opera.

Mom loved the opera, and Dad loved her; sometimes you just have to give a person credit for showing their love in the only way they know how.

⁂

As a girl in public school my social life revolved around three things—performing, going to the movies, and my friends in the Star Stamp Society.

As a child I was given dancing lessons—this was before the Crash—and I remember one performance in particular. I was doing a Spanish dance, and my costume was a red shawl. In the middle of the number, my costume fell off. I mean, the snap at the shoulder gave and the shawl came just completely down around my ankles, and there I stood, in front of a packed auditorium, in my panties and no top.

I was six or seven years old, and I was mortified. I remember running off into the wings and sobbing to my teacher, a man named

Jules; just sobbing and crying while he kept patting me and trying to tell me that it was all right.

Of course it wasn't all right!

I had appeared in public without my top and I couldn't see ever getting over the shame of it.

But I did.

The interesting thing about the story to me is just how quickly I did get over that costume fiasco. My rapid recovery doesn't make me think of myself as resilient; it makes me think of myself as tenacious: even at six or seven I knew that if I didn't get over my costume falling off of me I was never going to be able to perform in public again.

And I was not going to give up performing.

By the time I was ten years old, in school at P.S. 80, I was a hardened veteran of "declamation contests." Teachers would pick certain students for our ability to "declaim," and I was chosen frequently and assigned a poem to memorize and then perform.

Once I won second prize for reciting "Oh, Captain! My Captain!," a poem by Walt Whitman about Abraham Lincoln that has always moved me. But it wasn't really the poetry that stirred me at the time. I just loved getting up there and speaking. I suppose it took some courage to do it, but the budding performer in me overcame the fear. I liked being on stage, and I still do—I am in this respect a typical Leo. As I get older, I do get a little more nervous, and I have less stamina than I used to, but being in front of an audience still energizes me.

My brother and I were close at this time and shared many similar interests. We both loved art classes at school, especially drawing, but I gave up drawing in despair when I saw how much better my brother was at it than I.

Mom still played tennis occasionally, and even more occasionally she would take Lorenz and me along with her to the courts. We would prove how worthy we were to accompany her by being ball catchers.

Our big treat every week, though, was going to the movies on Saturday afternoons. Lorenz and I thought of this as a great luxury—an entire afternoon in the cool, dark expanse of a theater with Charlie Chaplin or the Marx Brothers! An afternoon free from both the toil of the shop where she worked and children underfoot must have seemed like a luxury to our mother too.

Lorenz loved the horror pictures, especially one called "The Mummy," which was made in 1932, but I didn't, because they scared me too much. I have never seen the point of scaring yourself silly, or why some people consider it entertaining to be frightened. What I loved was Rodgers and Hart, Fred Astaire and Ginger Rogers, musical comedy, singing and dancing and sophisticated people in glamorous clothes living in large, exquisitely appointed apartments. The movies is where I got the idea that I was going to be a singing, dancing star just like Ginger Rogers when I grew up.

Maybe it sounds odd—because, at that time, this hobby was associated mostly with boys—but what my friends and I did when we were in public school was collect stamps.

There were six of us—my best friend Bebe, and Annette, and Bella, and Bella's twin sister, and Joyce, and me—and we would get together at someone's house to compare and show off and paste our newest stamps into our collection books. We called ourselves the Star Stamp Society—the S.S.S.—and we even made ourselves little blue cotton jackets with the group's name on the breast pockets.

Maybe this will sound even more odd, but I didn't really like stamp collecting all that much.

What I liked were the six of us, all of my friends, together. I liked the feeling of belonging I had when I was with them, and I would have done whatever I had to do, even collect stamps, in order to be around these little girls.

I have not kept in touch with the members of the Star Stamp Society—time and circumstance have intervened—but during the dark days of the Depression, when my mother was working so hard and we had to go to court to fight with my father for money and my most constant companion was a little boy three and a half years my junior, these little girls were my family.

It's unusual, I think, to spend four years of your life in one place and have it leave so little an imprint on you, but I remember almost nothing from my high school years.

I went to an all-girls school, Walton, in the Bronx. I was an average student, lots of B's and low A's, so maybe a little above average. I didn't participate in many school activities, and I wasn't really even focused on the theater at the time, though it was quite clear to me that when I grew up I was going to be a famous actress. I was chosen by a teacher I liked very much to help him out in his classroom—cleaning up, recording scores in his grade book, that sort of thing—and I developed a bit of a crush on him because he was an exceedingly intelligent and very sweet man, but I can't recall his name. I think, perhaps, it was Mr. Schneider. Except for that crush, I didn't have any boyfriends—I mean, it was an all-girls school, remember, so there weren't a lot of boys in my world to have crushes on.

When I did find myself feeling that insistent pinprick of attraction we call a crush, I had no idea what to do about it. There was Nathaniel, a sweet, delicate sort of a boy from my neighborhood whose presence used to just delight me, make me giggle, and feel strange in my stomach; and there was Doris, blonde and chubby and possessed of something magical that drew me to her, but I had no idea how to act on these attractions.

My mother never explained to me how love might bud and bloom, much less about anything to do with sex itself.

I'm not faulting Mom; people didn't do that then. Really, they didn't explain much of anything to a kid. But I do have a few very interesting memories of sex.

I remember being three years old and playing with the little boy from the apartment next door who suggested that "if I showed him mine he would show me his," and I remember, distinctly, such a feeling of what seemed a lifetime of curiosity about to be satisfied.

I remember being five years old and the target of a flasher in the park; this was something that I had never even imagined seeing before—a grown man with his trousers unzipped!—and I remember feeling scared and confused—walking around with his trousers unzipped was something I knew a proper grown-up man just didn't do.

And I remember that I was six years old when my mother caught my two-and-a-half-year-old brother playing with himself.

I didn't witness the masturbation incident, but I had a very good little friend named Gracie who happened to be visiting me at the time the incident took place. Gracie's mother and mine were friends, so she was often in our home, and Gracie and I had a very warm connection ourselves—we told each other everything—but her whispered recounting to me of my mother's reaction to catching my brother fondling his genitals made me sick with fear. My mother had threatened that if she ever caught Lorenz doing that to himself again she was going to "cut his little thing off." I remember being scared to death.

Masturbation—or, as I have come to prefer to call it, self-pleasuring—is such an instinctive act. There is even evidence now of babies self-pleasuring in the womb. But self-pleasuring is not, to this day, presented to children in a positive way.

Children are not assured that it is a natural part of the exploration of self that is growing up. They are not taught that it is a sure-fire way of relieving teenage hormonal frustration and a responsible form of sexual release until they are ready to take on the responsibility of a partner. They are not encouraged to see it as a beautiful act of self-love and a satisfying part of the sexual repertoire of a mature person. After hearing how my mother reacted to it, I remember thinking that it was a fucking crime.

I have no memories of fondling myself at an early age, but, of course, I'm sure I didn't do it again ever after the incident with my brother. If my mother had admonished Lorenz about masturbation with the threat of homegrown genital surgery, I can only imagine the sort of severe reaction she might have had to a girl-child indulging in the same activity.

I'm sure I must have masturbated—it is so very natural for children to play with themselves—but I have no memory of it.

What I do know is that I consciously ignored a child's natural and innate curiosity about herself. I ignored the idea of the physical body altogether and became properly ignorant about sex. I became ignorant about sex to the point that one day, in 1934, when I was twelve years old and trying, in isolation, to piece together the little I had not been able to avoid knowing about sex, I decided that, if babies came from *down there*, they must come out through the ass.

Can I even tell you how horrifying that idea was?

Need I tell you?

I have gotten over my own ignorance and the outrage for all of the things I didn't know for all of those years; I understand that I was conditioned, and my mother was conditioned, by our times and the society we lived in. Educating children about even the most basic essentials of reproduction was unheard of in my time. I have never been able to come to grips with people who still, today, keep their own children in ignorance and thereby make them inheritors of the guilt and shame that is all that ignorance has ever fostered.

Even people about whom you would like to believe better can let you down when it comes to such an incendiary and taboo topic as masturbation. I was thrilled when our Surgeon General, Jocelyn Elders, at long last let a little light in on the topic by suggesting our children should no longer be made to feel ashamed for participating in an activity that children, and grown-ups too, have been participating in since the dawn of time.

I was furious when Bill Clinton's administration forced the resignation of this enlightened and visionary and oh-so-very-practical woman.

After I calmed down a bit, I sat down at my typewriter and composed a long and thoughtful letter to the president detailing the ways in which his administration had just compromised the sexual health of yet another generation.

The president never responded; I mean, not even a form letter acknowledging receipt of my effort to argue the case!

In the seventy-some years that have intervened between Lorenz's infamous masturbation incident and now, I have become, of course, a quite vocal advocate for self-pleasuring. Part of the reason I was able to grow into an appreciation for mature self-love is that I got very lucky. When I was eighteen I met my first boyfriend. He was tender and gentle and humble and enlightened. He showed me where my clitoris was and opened up for me all of the pleasure that was inside my body, just waiting there for me to take. I remember after a date, after the first time my boyfriend demonstrated to me the incredible potential of my clitoris, how I couldn't wait to get home and try it out again, for myself. I remember the feeling of joyous anticipation that preceded each date I had with this boy, knowing that the petting sessions that invariably were a part of our evenings together would end in rapturous release. I remember being so grateful that this boy had come into my life: I might have gone though all of my life without experiencing this divine, transcendent feeling if not for him!

Eventually, my boyfriend proposed marriage to me.

I was in love with him, but I turned him down.

I was going to be an actress.

You couldn't go into the theater if you had a husband.

Married ladies didn't have careers.

Chapter Four

Rape, Communism, and Other Unmentionables

I won't tell you his name.

What would be the purpose? It was so long ago. 1940.

I met him right away after high school, when I was invited to join a theater company at a local synagogue. I was one of the singers. I knew all the popular songs of the time, and I got to sing them on stage. I thought I was on my way via the synagogue to the Big Time.

Is there any person who walks with a lighter step than a kid just out of high school with her whole life before her?

I was living at home, so I had very few expenses to trouble me, and I was singing publicly to enthusiastic audiences, so I thought the path to my future career was laid out smoothly before me. Moreover, the theater company's comedian, who I liked a lot, had just asked me out on a date.

I liked this guy a lot because he was so very, very funny, and I have always been a sucker for a good punch line. When this comedian asked me to go with him to his college prom my small world became the absolute most perfect place there ever could be.

Now we would call it date rape.

The comedian date raped me on a sofa in a New York University student building after the prom and took my virginity.

I use the word *took* deliberately because I was not ready or willing to let anyone do that to me.

The comedian held me down on that sofa while I struggled and yelled, "No, No, No, No!"

But here is an example of what I mean when I say I was conditioned by the time and society I lived in: I was so very angry with the comedian, and I processed the ordeal as a gross violation, but I knew I shouldn't make a big deal out of it. I had gone out with this guy on a date and how could you accuse someone you willingly, even eagerly, spent time with of forcing himself on you?

I remember the next morning looking at myself in the mirror and thinking that while a very dramatic thing had just happened to me, I was not changed in any dramatic way; I still looked the same. No one I passed on the street would be able to look at me and point and say, "That girl's not a virgin." My mother wasn't going to be able to look at me over breakfast and know. The lingering physical pain was mine alone, minimal, and very private.

And my anger? Surely society was right? This very dramatic thing would not have happened had I not agreed to go out on a date with the comedian. It was my fault for saying "yes" at all. My anger at him was, of course, misplaced; I should be angry with *me*.

And I was.

Incredible as it may sound today, I believed that society would see me as being at fault for my rape. The blame would be placed primarily at my feet *because I accepted the offer of a date with him in the first place.*

Almost as overwhelming, however, as believing that if I talked about my rape I was the one who was certain to be censured for loose morals was the intense disappointment I felt about the act itself.

All my previous sexual experimenting—both petting with my high school boyfriend and masturbation—had led me to believe that actual intercourse was a thing from which I could expect physical pleasure both explosive and sublime.

The morning after my encounter with the comedian I remember looking at myself in the mirror and thinking, "Oh. Is that all there is?"

I didn't see the comedian again after that.

Not for over thirty years.

I left the synagogue's theater company soon after the incident with the comedian and started, like all New York actors, to make the rounds of auditions.

Claude Thornhill was a popular bandleader back then, and I heard that he was looking for a girl singer.

I was so nervous about the idea of auditioning for him that I decided to get all dressed up in the gown from my high school prom so I could make myself feel attractive and sophisticated and work up the courage to telephone him and ask to be seen. I laid it on thick when I finally got Mr. Thornhill on the phone. I told him that he ought to hear me sing because I was going to be the next Ginger Rogers.

But I'd heard wrong; Claude Thornhill wasn't looking for Ginger or me or anybody.

An agent came to see me perform and told me he wanted to represent me. He said he could make me into the next Mary Martin and he signed me up to participate in a radio competition. I prepared a song—"My Heart Belongs To Daddy," which, considering the relationship I had with my father, I have always thought of since as an odd and interesting choice—but, at the last minute, the radio station added some extra singers to the program and, by the time it was my turn to sing, the program was off the air.

I didn't become the next Mary Martin.

I didn't even sing that well for the judges in the studio because I knew my family and friends had gathered around their radios to hear me perform and I was so pissed off because I wasn't on the air.

Another agent. He told me he represented Peggy Lee, and he wanted to represent me, too.

If I would sleep with him.

I'd like to say that I didn't even consider the offer, but the lore about the old casting couch is very real and, anyway, it wasn't as if it was going to be my first time again, right?

In the end what got to me was the feeling that I would be betraying my first boyfriend and all the possibilities of all the great romances still ahead of me if I didn't dump this guy quick.

Years later it occurred to me that this agent was, of course, only trying to use my ambition to get what he wanted—sex—from me, and, had I not been what we called in those days a "nice girl," I could easily have used sex to get what I wanted from him. It occurred to me that, had I considered things from this perspective at the time the agent made me his sleazy offer, I might have exploited the power of sex I had over him to my own benefit.

I'm not saying that it would have been right of me to exploit this power—the misuse of power is what has gotten women and men into the mess the women's movement has long been trying to clean up. What I am saying is that, like other "nice girls" for a hundred generations before me, I didn't know I had any power at all.

The upshot, at the time, however, was that I didn't become the next Peggy Lee either.

No next Ginger Rogers, no next Mary Martin, no next Peggy Lee. It was slowly becoming clearer that maybe I was just supposed to be me.

Auditions were turning out to be a round of disappointments. Fortunately, I had a group of good friends around me, and a new boyfriend, who I was crazy about, to sustain me through the endless rejections.

My friends and I would take the train in the evenings to Greenwich Village, to go to the music clubs and hear performers like Josh White and, later, the Weavers. It was a particular thrill to be in the audience when Josh White was performing. Josh White was the first black artist to give a White House Command Performance, and he was the first to perform in previously segregated clubs and hotels. He was also one of the closest advisors to President Roosevelt on issues of black social reform—and his music was just transportingly wonderful too. Being in a Josh White audience seemed to heighten the excitement of an already thrilling time. My friends and I and, it seemed, everyone in Greenwich Village were young and socially aware and ready to change the world if only someone would tell us how. Josh White *was* changing the world.

The boy I was crazy about was named Peter. I guess I wasn't madly in love with him because I don't recall his last name, but he had such a cute, goyish face, and he wasn't so tall, which I appreciated as I am not so tall myself. I thought he was dashing but maybe that was only because he'd grown up in England and had the most appealing accent.

Peter and I had only a short time together, six months at the most. Our country had just entered World War II and he was in the Merchant Marine, due to ship out for duty. We made the most of the time we knew we would have together—we must have gone to the Village to nurse beers and listen to music almost every night—and then we said our goodbyes, he boarded his ship, and he was gone out of my life.

It was a wartime romance, lovely and purposefully frivolous, poignant and cut short. I didn't even suspect I was pregnant until Peter was somewhere out on the high seas, far away and unreachable.

For all of the frivolity of our brief affair, I knew I could have turned to Peter with the problem of my pregnancy had I had any idea of where he was. I do think that I wouldn't have, in any case, looked for him very hard. I was, in a way, relieved that he was no longer in the picture (i.e., that marriage wasn't an option), because I knew I wasn't ready to have a child.

I didn't know much of anything else, though, and I went to see one of Peter's best friends, a young man named Bert.

Bert was as sympathetic and supportive as Peter himself would have been. He found a doctor located somewhere in the 30s, off Park Avenue, who would perform the abortion in his office, and he arranged with Peter's parents to pay the mind-boggling sum of $500 for the operation.

Abortion was, of course, illegal at the time: I knew I was fortunate to be having the procedure done by a medical doctor and not by some back alley butcher; I knew I was fortunate to have the wherewithal to have the procedure done at all. I did not expect the pain.

The abortion was the most physically, shockingly painful event of my young life.

I was not given anesthetics for the procedure—an operation known as a "D&C" because the patient's cervix is *d*ilated and the tissues lining the uterus are *c*ut away. The doctor explained to me that anesthetics sometimes caused complications that could require hospitalization and, therefore, he wasn't going to jeopardize his practice or his reputation by taking the risk of me ending up in an emergency room. I was just going to have to suck up the unutterable pain the procedure would involve.

To say that I was terribly weak and shaky after the operation does not begin to cover the prolonged sensation of what seemed to be every individual organ inside of me being scraped clean. I took a taxi home and stumbled to my bed and curled up there and cried.

My mother came into my room and sat down on the bed beside me while I wept. What she said to me was startling—less for the compassion in the words and more for the clairvoyance of them— "If you would have come to me about this, I would have helped you."

I had thought that if my mother knew I was pregnant she would have been condemning, as most mothers at the time would have been, but she was completely reasonable about it. I think that was one of the reasons I was able to be, quite rapidly, reasonable about it myself.

I think it's important to talk at this point about a major and long-term regret I have in my life, and that is that I never had children, or, more precisely, that I was never able to get pregnant when I finally found someone with whom I wanted not only to have, but also to raise children.

I do not regret having had the abortion; it was absolutely the right thing to do at that time in my life. I mean, I think most women who get abortions don't really have their heart in it—no one is *pro-abortion*—but if a pregnancy happens when a woman isn't ready for it, abortion is a necessary option.

This issue is the sort of thing I can still sit up for hours and think about. If the right wing in this country is so fervently anti-choice, why do they oppose the sort of rounded and grounded sex education for young people that would keep them from having to make this hard choice at all? Wouldn't it better serve everyone's agenda if we gave up the pipe dream of populating the nation's high schools and colleges with virgins? Wouldn't it be better if we gave these kids the information they need about their bodies well in advance of them getting carried away by their bodies' natural and insistent and delicious sexuality so that they would not need to terminate an unwanted pregnancy? Wouldn't it be better if, instead of forcing children to have children, we did our best to make sure every child born was welcomed into a loving home?

This is the sort of thing that can still make me so angry that I can't sleep, and that motivates me to get up in the morning and tackle the work that I do with fresh energy and renewed purpose. Why are the young people of this country still left to flounder in ignorance about their perfectly natural sexual desire?

The short-term repercussions of my abortion? I vowed that never again would I experience such seething pain, and, so, I had myself fitted for a cervical cap and became as rigid about its use as I've been about anything in my life.

Then I rested for about three days, drank the hot soup my mother brought to me, and went back to work.

❧

I'd auditioned to be a part of a theater company called The Bronx Variety Players and was given a place in their cast. It was 1942. I was twenty years old by this time, and the Players had been created by a young woman close to my own age, Madeline Lee. Madeline has since had a long and successful marriage to the actor Jack Gilbert, and you can see her on TV in shows like *Law & Order, Mad About You,* and HBO's recent original movie, . . . *And Starring Pancho Villa as Himself.* Back then she was a radio performer, and her specialty was doing children's and babies' voices; her tiny voice belied big organizational abilities.

Madeline took a storefront on Jerome Avenue as the home for her players. From there she adapted scripts for our shows, rehearsed our company of six, and managed the day-to-day details of running a theater; she also, of course, took part in performances for the soldiers passing through New York who were training at the base in the Bronx and shipping out to Europe. I guess you could say that the Bronx Variety Players was a sort of small, private USO, although we weren't formally affiliated with that organization.

Our revues consisted of renditions of popular songs—sometimes with a verse or two of original lyrics that satirized a current event—comedic dance routines, and scathing political skits. Lorenz, who was about seventeen, was part of the cast of the Players too—our comedian. Lorenz had a brilliant, spontaneous sense of humor, and he was limber and loose, like Donald O'Connor, and could dance like him too. I remember one particular piece Lorenz did where he would stuff his costume full of pillows to make himself look fat and just skewer a certain right-wing Southern senator with a dead-on imitation.

Between our mother's influence and the encouragement of being around like-minded friends and colleagues, my brother and I had quite liberal leanings. The topical material we presented on stage every night reflected our own understandings and concerns about how the world was working—or, more accurately, in our views, was *not* working—and we played the material with heart. The social foment of the times, the energy of it that made our favorite haunts in the Village simply vibrate with optimism and idealism, was bound to lead us toward even more committed action than merely satirizing the status quo.

One action I took was to join the Communist Party.

Were it not for the bitter, utter fiasco that came years later—with the rise of Senator McCarthy and the House Un-American Activities Committee (HUAC), and all the careers that were destroyed and all the talent that was wasted (my hero, Josh White, being one of the sacrificed)—I suppose I could be amused at the misunderstanding that still, today, exists to some degree about us early Communists.

Let's clear something up: of course we were never aiming to overthrow the government of the United States. We were aiming to improve working conditions for the average working guy and gal.

Because my own career opportunities were later limited by my party membership, I can look back with honor at having been, even peripherally, in the company of the great writers, actors, directors, and producers who were blacklisted during the dark days of the McCarthy era—people such as Mr. Josh White, Dalton Trumbo, Ring Lardner, Jr., Charlie Chaplin, Lauren Bacall, Henry Fonda… how that list goes on!

But, more immediately relevant to the journey toward Eve's Garden that I'm writing about here, I look back at my involvement with the Communist Party as an important step on my spiritual path.

How so? Well, I refer you again to a book I have already recommended you read, *The Great Cosmic Mother*, and a riveting chapter in that book titled "Marx and the Matriarchy." I'll summarize here: Marx's famous quote about religion being the opiate of the people? Nobody ever gets that right. Or, at least, very few cite the whole of the quote and use his words in context.

What Karl Marx wrote was this:

Religion is at the same time the expression of real distress and the protest against real distress. Religion is the sigh of the oppressed creature, the heart of the heartless world, just as it is the spirit of a spiritless situation. It is the opium of the people. The demand to give up the illusions about its conditions is the demand to give up a condition that needs illusions. Criticism had plucked the imaginary flower from the chain, not so that men will wear the chain without any fantasy or consolation, but so that they will break the chain and cull the living flower.[6]

What Marx was protesting was not religion itself, but the way that mainstream religious organizations conspire with established political and economic institutions to keep the little guy, the working guy and gal, within their control. He was pointing out how a small elite group of powerful men use religion as a tool to keep the worker drones focused on the rewards of heaven rather than on the lot they endure *to the benefit of that small elite* here on earth. What Marx made those of us who recognized ourselves as worker drones yearn for was not the dissolution of religion or political organizations as we knew them, for its own sake, but a renewal of *spirit*. *Heart*. We ached not for the divinity of religious icons that could make us tremble with awe and fear, but for the humanity of them that could release us to celebrate our own humanity.

The mistake Marx made was in assuming that the mainstream *religious* organizations of the day represented some sort of *spiritual* pinnacle. In retrospect, of course, it's easy to see this basic error—I'm not saying we weren't all terribly naïve—but being exposed to what I guess I would call now a primitive quest for some more integrated and fulfilling way of life helped to set me on my own path toward that potential.

So? What was the next career move this particular Commie made?

I joined the United States Army.

---

[6] Karl Marx, *Critique of Hegel's Philosophy of Right*; quoted by Christopher Hitchens, "Laying to Rest Beliefs on Religion and Politics," *In These Times 8,* no. 2 (November 16, 1983): 27.

Chapter Five

Tec 4 Dell Zetlin

I enlisted in the army in 1945; my army days were among the happiest of my life.

Because of my experience in the theater, I was classified as an Entertainment Specialist, and was stationed to Northington General Hospital in Tuscaloosa, Alabama. The hospital was a sprawling place, twenty or thirty buildings, a way station where our soldiers who'd been wounded in Europe were funneled back into civilian life. From Northington General, they were either admitted to a more specialized hospital for continued medical treatment or discharged and sent home.

The officer I reported to was a major, in charge of entertainment for the entire hospital complex, and from the beginning it was clear that he and I were not destined to be the best of friends. Though I am a tiny person, the job he assigned to me was to roll around a huge wheeled platform stage with a piano on it to various wards all over the hospital complex so that two civilian singers and their accompanist could entertain the soldiers.

I am a tiny person with a lot of muscle. Besides, I was a soldier now too, and I rather took a little pride in being asked to do a job that would ordinarily be assigned to a man. This is not to mention the pride I took in being able to pull off the physical stunt of shuttling that platform around in front of the major—showing off to him just how poorly he'd miscalculated my determination. I didn't complain about the work I was required to do. What I complained about were the singers.

They were terrible. The soprano, in particular, was merciless, and the group didn't have any popular songs in their repertoire, which was what the patients really wanted to hear.

At the end of my first week on the job, I marched into the major's office and told him, "Look, I don't mind about having to move the piano, but those two singers just aren't good enough to entertain our troops. These men have already been wounded enough." I told him what he ought to do was to call upon some of the members of the company who had real experience in show business—there were enough of us—to pull together a really bang-up revue.

I am a tiny person with a big mouth.

The next day I found myself transferred out of Entertainment and into Legal, where I was deposited into the clerical pool.

Eventually I got lucky again. I got myself assigned to the office in charge of the Morning Report.

Every company in every branch of the service had to have a Morning Report— who has shown up to perform what duty, who's been transferred in and who's been processed out. This report was sent to Washington, D.C. where all of the service people in the entire armed forces were accounted for on a daily basis, so it was important paperwork, but in its essence it was really just an attendance record. Still, there was a specific format and protocol that had to be followed. The guy who I learned the job from showed me all the ropes and, when he was transferred out of Northington General, I was tapped as his replacement.

What a great deal! Nobody could tell me how to do my job anymore because nobody else really knew how to do it. I got promoted from Private to Sergeant (I liked that!) and I got my own assistant. Moreover, once the report was filed for the day, my time was my own.

In the free time I now had, I got together with two other enlisted men and we wrote, produced, and performed in a daily radio show that was broadcast over the hospital's station. I was the only woman in this little group, and the only one who knew how to type, so I'd sit at the typewriter and the three of us would throw ideas around until we came up with a good comic situation we could improvise around, and then I'd get it down on paper—like on the television show, *The Dick Van Dyke Show.* I was the "Sally" to my colleagues "Rob and Buddy."

Our comedy was in the style of the then-popular *The Bob and Ray Show* radio program that mimicked the frailties of the human condition. We called the show *Our Day,* after Eleanor Roosevelt's widely read syndicated daily newspaper column, "My Day." It was just a fifteen-minute show, but the patients loved it. The on-duty staff would stop for a break when it came on the air so they could also listen to it. The show made little celebrities out of my two partners and me.

Inspired by my time on the radio show, I toyed for a while with the idea of becoming a comedy writer—maybe for that new medium, television, which everyone was saying was only going to get more popular as the years went on—but the pleasure of being in front of an audience made the solitary life of a writer pale in comparison.

I auditioned to be the "girl singer" in the hospital band that entertained our troops, and I got the job. The hospital staff put together variety shows and performed them in the wards. I couldn't volunteer fast enough to be a part of them.

I'd put in for overseas duty when I first signed up with the army. While I was at Northington General I was finally advised that I should prepare to ship out. The boys in the hospital band threw a farewell party for me—food and flowers, beer and my boys (and their dates!)—and then, almost as soon as my orders came through, they were canceled. Wacs were no longer being sent out of the country.

I felt a little sheepish in not leaving after all the effort the fellows had put into making my leave-taking a memorable one, but when I walked into band rehearsal the next day to see if they still wanted me to sing with them, there was a huge sign over the bandstand—"SHE'S BACK!" The little bit of trouble they took to make that sign still touches me as a big acknowledgment of the friendship we shared.

When Northington General closed down, I was transferred to Oliver General Hospital in Augusta, Georgia.

Oliver General had been an elegant hotel before it was converted into a hospital during the war, and there was still evidence of elegance in its architecture, underneath all of the army-issue medical and clerical equipment. The old hotel boasted a pretty good golf course, too—what is now Augusta National Golf Course, home of the Masters Tournament, and you'd better believe the officers took full advantage of this perk! It was a beautiful place to be stationed, even if I could never quite get it out of the back of my mind that if I'd tried to enter its grand rooms as a paying customer before the United States got into the war they wouldn't have let me in: no blacks or Jews or women were allowed as members.

To this day, I can't recall what my regular job was at Oliver General—I assume it was so dull I simply forgot it—but my extracurricular activities will stay in my memory always. It was at Oliver General Hospital that I met First Lieutenant Mary B. Winslow and became involved in the culminating, crowning experience of my army career.

Lieutenant Winslow had operated the Monomoy Theater on Cape Cod in her civilian life, and now she wanted to create an original Wac-produced musical and perform it at the hospital. She held open auditions and I signed up immediately.

The show was called *Call Me Mrs.* The title alone should give you some idea of how politically incorrect it was. It was about two Wacs and the one G.I. they were vying to trap into marriage. I got two roles in the show—neither of the star Wacs in question, but the Sarge, Breathless, and another quite comedic character named Daisy Bumps—the comic relief.

The highlight of the show—the part that brought the house down every time it was performed—was a number I did with two other women. We paraded onto the stage dressed as cleaning women, carrying buckets and mops, and performed a song called "When I Begin to Clean the Latrine," to the tune of Cole Porter's "Begin the Beguine." The calls of "Encore!" that little song provoked, I have to say, spoiled all three of us.

The show's original run was scheduled for just one night, but that night the woman who was the commander of the Wac detachment in the Southern Region just happened to be on base. She was invited to be in our audience, and she loved the show. She decided to send us on the road with it.

Talk about a long, strange trip!

We set out in a big, old G.I. bus we dubbed "Bertha," with a crew of eleven, an orchestra of six, and a cast of thirty-five (including a duck named "Junior"). We traveled to eight different army and navy bases, covering over 2,700 miles, in a little less than two months. We carried our scenery, lighting (including a dimmer board that never worked exactly right), and costume trunks with us, and we got so proficient with the equipment we could set the whole show up on a new stage in under two hours and tear it down and repack to move to the next venue in less than one. We repaired the sets on the way to a new location, as best we could, and when the beds we were using as part of our stage set started to look too shabby, the Red Cross replaced them for us! We kept improving the show along the way—adding jokes or new lyrics to songs or, at least, I did, and I must have been insistent about it. Lieutenant Winslow typed up her director's notes and handed them out to us as a souvenir of our trip and I reread them recently. There are several exasperated notations, "Dell wants to change that song *again*." We performed on indoor stages and in outdoor arenas. We got rained out, rained on, and lost once or twice getting to where we were supposed to go. We entertained over 20,000 G.I.'s and showed them, I think, at least as good a time as we were all having.

When we got back to Oliver General, we all got Letters of Commendation from the Surgeon General for our participation in *Call Me Mrs.*, and, shortly thereafter, I got a notice from the same office that my hitch in the army was over. I had to sign up again or go home. The war was over at this point, victory had been declared and everyone, including me, was looking forward to getting back to our families. Still, it was wrenching. I mean, how do you say goodbye to a group of people you've loved so much you could live with them on a bus for two months?

The spirit of camaraderie among the people I served with at both Northington General and Oliver General was terrific, like nothing I had experienced before or would again, until I got involved in the women's movement in the early 1970s.

Chapter Six

Leonard

Sometimes I forget I've told someone a particular story and they remind me when I start to tell it again. Or, sometimes I can't remember a phone number I call nearly every day or whether I've taken my vitamins in the morning. This doesn't happen often, and it's not the sort of thing that doesn't happen to everybody now and again. I don't blame it so much on being 82.

What does happen with age, though, when you have such a full life, is that some things get buried at the back of your brain—like when you finally clean out your closet and find a favorite old dress you thought you gave to Goodwill years ago. Sometimes the things that get buried are important.

My brother, Lorenz, enlisted in the army at about the same time I did. He had been touring in a show called *Junior Miss* prior to joining up, and he had an agent who said he was going to make him the next Donald O'Connor. (It may seem as if, in recounting the stories of all these agents who told my brother or me that they were going to make one or the other of us into the next *whoever* that agents back in those days weren't too original, but, you know for sure, someone's out there right now pitching some kid as the next Britney Spears.)

My brother's agent arranged to get him a screen test—a big break. The screen test ended up being scheduled on the day before Lorenz was due to report for duty. He took the test, and then he shipped out.

Years later, when he got back home, though the same agent pursued him as a client, Lorenz never did follow up about an acting career—he came back from the war with other, newer dreams—but, in my opinion, the entertainment world lost out; his talent was that big.

In the army, Lorenz was an Entertainment Specialist too, like me, and he was stationed in the Panama Canal. My brother and I wrote to each other often when we were in the service, long letters. I recently found a stack of his letters to me and I reread them. They're funny and touching and full of typos.

He wrote to me about the stuff soldiers commonly write about—bad food, and long days, and missing home. He wrote about the musical pieces he was performing— he told me about a piece he did, a Carmen Miranda impersonation in full costume, bananas on his head and everything; he said that he was improving it with every performance and it was the funniest thing, and I completely trusted his word on that—he'd debuted the Carmen Miranda act with the Bronx Variety Players, and I remember how smashing even the original, unimproved version had been.[7]

In one letter, dated May 9, 1946, Lorenz wrote to ask me if I'd gotten any letters recently from that fiancé of mine. He wrote that he didn't think any guy was good enough for his big sister. He said I was going to make that fiancé of mine one lucky guy.

I hope brothers still send their sisters letters like that but, here's the thing: I had forgotten that I had a fiancé.

His name was Leonard Czajozynski. I met him while I was performing with the Bronx Variety Players, and he was one of the soldiers at the station the army maintained at NYU. He came into

---

[7] Years later I saw Mickey Rooney do a Carmen Miranda imitation on television. Sorry, Mickey, but my brother's Carmen was twice as funny as yours.

the canteen one Saturday night and that was pretty much it for us. It was the sweetest time we had together, for two months, until he was shipped overseas. He wrote to me from wherever he was stationed in Europe, and I wrote back; he proposed to me in a letter, and I answered back, "Yes."

It wasn't until 1946 that I saw Leonard again. I'd joined the army myself, served my hitch, and been discharged all in the time since we'd last laid eyes on each other. He was home on leave, waiting for his own discharge papers to be processed. We arranged to meet under the clock at the Hotel Biltmore.

I got to the hotel early on the appointed day; I was so nervous, waiting for him to come. This was a man I'd been engaged to for over a year but had only really gotten to know in letters. What would we talk about? Would we talk as easily together as we wrote to each other? Would I have that feeling of love when I saw him again? How would I know if I did? What *did* that feeling of love feel like?

I was genuinely and overwhelmingly glad to see Leonard when he appeared beside me under the clock.

I guessed that was the feeling I'd been waiting for.

Leonard had taken a room at the Biltmore, and he asked me to go there with him, and I did.

Perhaps Leonard's original intent in taking the room had been only so that we would have a place to be alone together, to get to really know each other again, some place out of the way of the milling crowd in the lobby. But, in that little room, Leonard and I made love together for the first time.

The next morning, after we parted in the hotel lobby, I never saw him again.

I've always thought that what turned Leonard off was that I let him make love with me, that he thought I was, as they said then, a "loose woman." I don't mean that he was offended that I'd had sex before I met him—I had not kissed and told; I mean that my having sex with *him* had been a too modern and independent thing for me to do. I wasn't a traditional enough sort of girl for him. It was all right for him to try to talk me into sleeping with him, but it wasn't all right for me to give in to his pleading.

It wasn't all right for me to have sexual desire as unbearably urgent as his.

All these years later, whenever I remember Leonard, the suddenness of our ending hits me all over again, and I feel an intense longing. I tried to look him up once, years ago; I found out he'd become a teacher, a college professor, but I never did come up with the courage to contact him directly. It's probably not so modern or independent to admit that I still think I would have loved being married to such a very traditional man. But it's the truth.

Recently, I dug out all the letters Leonard ever wrote to me, reread them, and relived our brief, long-distance love affair. It was a most difficult exercise. And it's probably why, most of the time, I forget that I loved him at all.

Chapter Seven

Hooray for Hollywood

Life after the army was a letdown, a depressing time for me. I missed the friends I'd made there, and I missed the constant, consuming participation in activities that were creative, demanding, and productive. I missed, moreover, the whole atmosphere that existed throughout our country during the war.

I mean, the war itself was, of course, a terrible thing, but there was a spirit alive in the country because of the war, a sense of sacrifices made gladly to achieve a noble goal, which could not be sustained as the postwar boom began. There was no longer a feeling that you were one with your neighbor, linked by a common purpose in the coming good times as you had been in the hard, recent past; you were just out for yourself now.

I had moved to the East 80's, in Manhattan, into a fourth-floor walk-up with a shared bath down the hall. It wasn't the first time I'd lived alone, but I had just come out of a situation of living so long and intimately with eleven other women in a barracks that our menstrual cycles had synchronized, and I was lonely.

I missed Leonard, and I was nursing my broken heart.

My mother was even more depressed than I was at the end of the war. Her brother, Simon, with whom she'd lived when she first immigrated to Paris, had disappeared during the German occupation of France. She was never to hear from him again. I think it was her morbid speculations about the fate of her beloved brother that, more than anything else, accounted for her progressively disconnecting from life.

I took a job as a secretary. I don't even remember the nature of the product of the company where I was employed much less the company's name. I do remember that the work was rote and unabsorbing.

I was still interested in the theater and had aspirations to be an actress, but I lacked the energy to pursue the auditions that might have gotten me work. For a time after my stint as a secretary had blessedly come to an end, I signed up for unemployment with the thought that I would now have time to make the rounds again, but I just ended up with too much time on my hands.

I volunteered to help at a veteran's organization, one that was created after World War II and that had a more progressive agenda than the American Legion. The people I knew and lived among, my family and friends, were always involved in some way with the fight for justice and equality, and I think I might have found the energy to go to work for this good organization simply because it was expected of me to give time to one cause or another. I did meet a couple of fellow actors at the veteran's office who were trying to put a musical comedy act together, but the funniest thing to come out of that effort was the memory of the slapstick that ensued on the day the movers came to install the piano I'd rented for our rehearsals in my tiny fourth-floor room. The stairs were too narrow to maneuver the piano, so the movers had to get a crane to hoist the instrument through my window. Then they had to remove the window in order to get the piano to fit through it—it was a real production, so to speak, both opening and closing night of our act, as it turned out.

My friend, Ginny, who I'd served with in the army and

who'd been with me in the cast of *Call Me Mrs.*, came to visit me in the city. We had a great time together, two women living in a small room with that big piano. And then Ned arrived. Ned had been the trumpet player in the army band at Oliver General, and Ginny's boyfriend. The moment Ginny and Ned saw each other again they rushed into each other's arms; it was one of the loveliest and most spontaneous outbursts of real love I have ever witnessed. Ned was still panting from running up the four flights of stairs to get to Ginny's arms, but he proposed to her on the spot.

In retrospect, I realize that I had a big crush on Ginny myself. She was a beautiful woman inside and out—quiet and lovely. If Ned had not proposed to her when he did, I often wonder if I might have discovered my inherent bisexuality much earlier than I did. At the time I was devastated at the loss of Ginny as my roommate, and the love she shared with Ned just made me think about Leonard, and ache.

What pulled me up and back into life again was the opportunity of a ride to California. A friend of mine was going to go out there to try his chances in Hollywood. He'd hired a couple to drive his car across the country for him, and, he said, I might as well go along with them because the back seat was just going to be empty if I didn't.

It was 1949. We set off on Route 66, headed west.

California!

When we got to Los Angeles, I called up the number my friend had given me before I set out. It was the phone number of a girl he knew who'd offered to share her apartment with me when I arrived. I moved in and set off at full gallop. I spent just a little over two years in Hollywood and I think I packed every day full.

Because I could rely on the G.I. Bill to afford the tuition, I decided to further my education. I auditioned for a place at the Actor's Laboratory Theater; it's a very prestigious school, so I was overjoyed when they accepted me. Morris Carnovsky, an actor for whom I had great respect, was the director of the Actor's Lab at that time, and his wife, Phoebe Brand, taught there too; it was a thrill to have them as my teachers.

I worked with an Improv Group that included such notables as Tony Curtis and Harry Guardino. I remember we were assigned monologues to rehearse and perform for the group, and I chose Hamlet's soliloquy—"To be or not to be . . ."—for my piece; the idea of presenting Hamlet as a woman, and the way such a gender change would nuance the reading, struck me as appealing.

While I'd been crazy about the theater, and the movies, all my life, I was never particularly star struck; proof of this came on the evening we presented our monologues to the class. One of my fellow students, a really outstandingly gorgeous woman who, I had been advised, was already a pretty big star, walked up to me and commented on my performance. "Gee," she said, "I wish that I could act as well as you can." Turns out I was talking to Piper Laurie.

I studied diction with determination; I honed my skills at dialects, and, while I was at it, I left behind my native Bronx accent at the Actor's Lab.

I got my equity card during this period, and some decent parts in a few plays in what could be considered Los Angeles's equivalent of off-Broadway—a show called *Parlor, Bedroom & Bath* in 1949, and one called *Fabulous Invalid* in 1950—but no movie roles. It was hard to get into the movies; pretty much everyone I saw offered me the casting couch as a way inside, but I wasn't going to go there again no matter how juicy the acting parts were.

To earn my living, I'd signed up as a secretary with a temporary agency. One day the agency called for me to go to a job at ABC—the woman who held the job permanently was on jury duty—and I found myself in the almost unbelievably enviable position of being Norman Corwin's assistant.

Norman Corwin was a radio writer, at the very top of his profession. He was the first to use radio with political awareness. In 1941, he'd written and produced *We Hold These Truths,* for CBS, an all-star celebration of the Bill of Rights' 150th anniversary, a program of such magnitude, and so finely executed, that it was aired on all four existing networks simultaneously. Mr. Corwin created the special V-E Day broadcast, *On a Note of Triumph.* Carl Sandburg called it "one of the all-time great American poems." Three months later he wrote *14 August,* a V-J documentary narrated by Orson Welles. When I met him, he'd just left CBS to produce a documentary for United Nations Radio in honor of that institution's tenth anniversary.

I didn't know I was to work with Norman Corwin until I reported for work on my first day, but when I was told the news I was as nervous and excited to meet him as I have been about meeting anybody in my life—and I have since had the pleasure of meeting some pretty famous people! I wasn't sure I would be able to act like myself or function normally in the presence of what I considered such greatness, but Norman Corwin stood up to receive *me* when I was shown into his office. I remember he was in his shirtsleeves, and he had on suspenders and a red necktie. He held out his hand to me and said, "Good morning, Miss Zetlin, I'm Norman."

"Please, call me Dell," I replied, and shook his hand eagerly.

Can I tell you what a terrific guy he was? Norman insisted that although we'd put each other on a first name basis, the rest of his staff, which was made up mostly of men, should continue to call me "Miss Zetlin." Or, rather, he didn't *insist*, but there is a natural sort of elevation in conduct that occurs when you are around people who are so deeply and genuinely respected, and respectful; nothing was forced, Norman was simply, deeply, and genuinely, a gentleman. The people who worked for him were in awe, and, because I worked so closely at his side, the deference they showed to him was extended to me. It was a deference I had never experienced before, and certainly of the kind that was unusual for women of that day—these men didn't merely open doors for me or stand when I entered a room. They listened to my suggestions about how to improve upon the work we were doing, accepted my opinions as credible, and acted on them.

I had lucked into a fascinating job, and I had a ball with it. Norman made me feel that I was indispensable, that we were a team; he'd ask me to take care of something in a way that made me feel I was so competent, and I'd run off to make sure it was done immediately and exactly, sometimes even anticipating what he wanted—I was learning to think like Norman Corwin!

Lots of big stars, like Charles Laughton and Van Heflin, narrated the various segments of Norman's documentary , and I got to sit in the booth with Norman as he directed. He could make his cast do whatever it was he wanted them to do so easily—as he inspired me to perform to the very best of my abilities—because he asked for things in such a quiet, gentle, supportive way.

On the day that Charles Laughton was to narrate a certain segment of the United Nations documentary, Norman sent me to meet him and escort him to the studio. As we walked together, Mr. Laughton and I passed the studio where the television show *Queen for a Day* was being taped.

Queen for a Day was a sort of Jerry Springer show of its time. The premise was that several ordinary women would stand on stage and compete in telling the sad stories of their lives. The one whose story was the most pathetic would be crowned "queen" and win a lot of prizes. I, personally, had never watched the show, but considering the plight of most women's lives prior to the women's rights movement, the stories must have been sad indeed—and universal enough to strike a real chord with the public: mobs of women attended the tapings and, of course, the home audience was huge.

As Mr. Laughton and I walked toward the studio where Norman was taping that day, he leaned toward me and whispered his sardonic comments about *Queen for a Day* as if I alone would be able to understand the depth and pattern of his thinking. The remarkable thing about what he was whispering to me was that he never once put down the sad women on the stage who were telling their sorry stories, though that was the way most critics of the show approached their dislike for it. Mr. Laughton's comments were about the idea of the show itself and the state of the culture that could foster such a display. I wish I had kept a diary and written those comments down so I could type them up and send them off to Jerry Springer today!

The United Nations radio show was called *DOCUMENT A/777*.[8] Document A/777 is the index number of The Declaration of Human Rights that had been adopted by the General Assembly of the United Nations. Part of Norman's show was a dramatic and powerful reenactment of the original roll call of the countries now willing to comply with these articles, juxtaposed with examples of injustices perpetrated against humankind in the past. Norman's

---

[8] You can obtain your own copy of this magnificent document by calling the United Nations at (800) 253-9646.

opening remarks will give you an idea of the immense impact of this document: "There is a man-made force thousands of times greater than the hydrogen bomb. It's an instrument of many parts, small, it can fit into a handbag yet it has the power to penetrate to the very core of human life. Details may be found in Document A/777."

The show was taped, but the broadcast had a "live" premier—the audience was filled with celebrities dressed in their red carpet best, gathered to listen. The premiere was what you would call today a real "A-List" event. During the premiere, I was standing in the back of the auditorium, next to Norman, shivering with feelings of patriotism and pride, listening to the broadcast begin: "United Nations Radio, in cooperation with the Mutual Broadcasting System, presents *DOCUMENT A/777*, written, directed, and produced by Norman Corwin, with the participation of the following international cast of stars of the film, stage, and radio: Richard Basehart, Charles Boyer, Lee J. Cobb, Ronald Coleman, Joan Crawford, Maurice Evans, Jose Ferrer, Reginald Gardner, Van Heflin, Jean Hersholt, Lena Horne, Marsha Hunt, Alexander Knox, Charles Laughton, Sir Laurence Olivier, Vincent Price, Edward G. Robinson, Robert Ryan, Hilda Vaughn, Emilyn Williams, and Robert Young."

Just then, a figure appeared on the stage, a shadow behind the curtain, a woman who was moving awkwardly, clearly unsure of where she was supposed to be.

Though we were well into the performance and the figure on stage was a singular distraction for the gathered celebrities and other VIPs, Norman turned to me quickly and calmly asked, "Could you please run back there and help that woman find her way?" And so, I did. I went backstage and escorted Joan Crawford, who'd arrived late and couldn't find her seat, into the audience.

Miss Crawford was so apologetic to me about her mistake,

as if she were a little girl who'd disobeyed. I remember thinking, "This is Joan Crawford?" She was so well known for being willful and spoiled and arrogant, so her humbleness was completely unexpected. I don't know if she has just gotten a bad rap from the press all these decades and really was easier to work with than she has been portrayed, but I do know I was sure at the time that it had to be Norman's influence that had tamed even this imperious star and made her behave.

Jury duty ran long for the woman who was Norman's permanent assistant, and I ended up working for him throughout the production of the series. It was, without a doubt, the finest working relationship I have ever had.

⚜

Another thing I did to make money while I was living in Los Angeles was to work as an artist's model, and I lucked into that good job too. The girl with whom I was rooming was an artist's model, and one day she was sick and couldn't make it in. She asked me if I would take her place.

The acting work I was getting paid very little, and I was quickly going broke; artists' models made eight dollars a day—big money for the time! I said, sure, I'd give it a try, though I'd never done it before. I mean, if knowing absolutely nothing about how to produce a documentary hadn't kept me from being an able and appreciated assistant to the great Norman Corwin, what was going to keep me from striking a few poses for some art students?

I knew very well when I set off for the studio that day that artists' models worked in the nude, but that was the only thing I was sure of.

"Have you ever done this before?" the instructor asked me,

and I thought he might be referring to my being unaware of the expected nudity.

"Yes," I lied bravely. "At the Art Student's League, in New York."

"Can you do two minutes?" he continued.

I figured out immediately what he meant and nodded. To be an artist's model, you have to strip down, ascend to a platform, and strike a pose there that you hold for two to three minutes while you are sketched, until the instructor calls out for you to change. The early dance training I had in New York came in handy in sustaining imaginative poses, but this wasn't exactly difficult work, in any case, unless you got yourself into a terribly uncomfortable position or the room was cold or you had a particularly paltry inner life and bored easily. But that first day I was terrified at being naked in front of so many strangers and even more scared that someone would see how badly my knees were shaking with fear and call me out as a fraud.

It turned out that someone *did* notice my shaking but, because the room *was* cold, the instructor just thought I was freezing and brought out an electric space heater for me.

After a week of substituting for my sick girlfriend, the teacher asked me if I'd like to come back to pose again. "Sure," I told him, and we negotiated a flat thirty-five-dollar-a-week fee for my services. I was pleased to have found such steady and lucrative work.

The teacher of that class was Ricco LaBrun, an artist himself, of course, and one whose work I had admired a great deal.

It's always such a perk when you get to meet and work with people whose own work has moved or inspired you, and that has been an ongoing blessing for me in the course of my life.

Romance, on the other hand, has not always been such a blessing.

During my time in Los Angeles I had several love affairs—a brilliant one with George Anthiel, the composer of *Symphonie Mechanic,* that was too brief, and a bitter one with a teacher of mine, Bob, that went on for much too long.

George, first.

He was in his late sixties when we met—more than forty years my senior—a physically unattractive man by anyone's standards. He was, simply put, short and ugly, but he had a magnetic personality. He lived life with such exuberance and grace that when we broke up (as we were bound to do; he was already married and was forthright about having no intention of leaving his wife), I couldn't really be too blue about it. I felt he gave me some of his joie de vivre to keep for the rest of my days.

Now, Bob.

I had enrolled to take singing lessons at a music school, and Bob was assigned as one of my instructors. Bob was older than I was by about ten years, but he pursued me like an eager, young boy. I wasn't really interested in him, at first, but he came after me relentlessly.

Was I in love with Bob, or is it just too hard not to believe you're head over heels for someone who courts you with such charm and intensity? I know that our sex life was joyous—that I looked forward eagerly every evening to falling into his arms to play.

Bob, like George, was already married; unlike George, he was equivocal about his matrimony.

Bob led me to believe, time and again and in so many ways, that when he and his wife finally divorced, he and I were going to have a long and happy and playful future together. He went so far as to rent an apartment and ask me to move in with him. The inference, to me, was clear.

But then Bob's wife, from whom he was separated, began to

telephone him at our apartment to discuss matters concerning their children, and their relationship.

Bob and his wife had two children together, so it was by all means legitimate that they would need to talk together frequently, but the content of their conversations always centered on the two of them reconciling.

I was very young, and the telephone calls made me physically sick with insecurity. I told Bob that it was time for him to finalize the divorce he had assured me had been inevitable since before he and I had even met.

I saw Bob off to Las Vegas, where he was going to take up residency for the several weeks required to get a divorce in Nevada. I stayed in Los Angeles and concentrated all my energies on fixing up the apartment where we were going to continue to live together after he returned, and to make it into a home.

Then Bob appeared at the door of our home a few weeks too early—two weeks shy of the time I knew he needed to have spent in Nevada in order to make his divorce legal. Bob told me he'd returned to California early because he wasn't yet ready to completely break off with his wife. He told me I should be patient with him until he was ready. He asked me to continue in our current arrangement until he felt both he and his wife were emotionally ready for divorce, but it was clear to me that Bob wasn't going to get a divorce at all. I had the good sense to summon the courage to break off with him.

Maybe I wasn't all that in love with Bob because summoning good sense when it comes to matters of the heart is probably one of the more difficult accomplishments of a lifetime, and breaking off with Bob didn't seem as wrenching to me as I thought it should be. Or, perhaps, it was my insecurity that strengthened my resolve to show him the door.

And then I saw Bob again, just days after our breakup, out

with *another* girl, not his wife either.

"*You dirty rat,*" I thought, and my body all but doubled over at this evidence of his perfidy.

I had to leave the music school and find another teacher because the possibility of running into Bob on a regular basis was too painful. However sensibly I had acted, I did it with a heart that was raw and sorrowful, as filled with jealousy over Bob's new girlfriend as, I supposed, his wife's was filled with jealousy over me.

I think, though, that a good thing came from my heartbreak over Bob: I learned to listen to other people's stories of loss in love, failure of connection in relationships, and tragedies of misplaced or misused affection, with an open and nonjudgmental heart. A course of action that seems sensible to an outsider isn't always possible, at least immediately, for the afflicted, and everyone has been afflicted in some way, at one time or another, by love. My sadness at losing Bob was complicated and exacerbated by my understanding of the grief he—and through him, *I*—had caused his wife. I actually began to feel sorry for her—that she was the one who ended up stuck with the cheating bastard—clearly Bob was incapable of being honest with either one of us! How foolish I had been to let Bob catch me up in his charade, and how lucky I had been to escape before I had two children by him and also wound up dependent on him. I often wished I could have found the courage to call up Bob's wife and talk to and apologize to her. But whether you'll ever know another person's story—whether you'll know her well enough so that she feels safe in telling it to you—maybe or maybe not; but everyone's got at least one story that, if you heard it, would touch you to the core and make you cry.

I learned this and I was able, over the years, to apply this knowledge to Bob too, to see him as having been afflicted, in his own way, and to forgive.

One of the things that happened to me while I was in Los Angeles—a thing that was to be part of the foundation of Eve's Garden and so have one of the most far-reaching influences in my life—was to walk by a bookstore one spring day in 1949 and browse through a little rack of books sitting on the sidewalk in front of the store.

I can't resist books. I guess I've always been greedy about them. I can never have too many, and I'm frequently reading three or four of them at the same time. That day, on that little outside rack, my eyes honed in on a book called *The Function of the Orgasm*,[9] by Wilhelm Reich.

The title alone fascinated me, of course—someone was writing about orgasm, actually putting that titillating word down on paper and then putting other words around and around it and making a whole book about it! I had to have this book for my own. I grabbed it up and rushed inside to buy it.

When I got back to my room, I opened the book immediately and began to devour it. It was an easy read. By that I mean that what Reich was saying about orgasm, though revolutionary, made so very much common sense. His ideas spoke to me, as though the author were right there, talking to me and touching my soul.

"The sexual process," Reich wrote, "i.e., the expansive process of biological pleasure, is the productive life process per se."

Sexuality is the creative force that governs life, according to Reich.

Orgasm, he explained, is composed of electrically charged

---

[9] *The Function of the Orgasm*, Wilhelm Reich. I write here a bit about what Reich had to say but I do it in my own words; his book is as worthy and exciting a read now as it was then, and I can't urge you strongly enough to pick it up.

energy that is raised and heightened in the course of lovemaking and, at the very pinnacle of orgasm, the energy is released into the universe.

He said that when a person reaches the height of sexual ecstasy, he is as one with his most creative, truest, self.

And I understood.

The feeling that you have when you're enjoying sex, that energy, approximates the movement of waves in the ocean. The waves of energy wash through your body and, when you reach shore and splash down, that is orgasm. The energy of orgasm is part of the rhythm of the earth, part of the earth itself, rings of water rushing and circling over each other and expanding outward one upon the other, a spiral that never ends.

The ancients who had likened sexual energy to concentric rings, and conceived as sacred symbols seashells with their own rings and spirals, had understood this flow of energy. The ancients had understood, Reich wrote, but we, in the millennia since, had forgotten to understand. We had disconnected from our oneness with the earth we live upon. We no longer respected its rhythms, and that was why we were polluting and pillaging our earth and each other. We must now, modern and well into the twentieth century as we were, remember.

And I *did*.

I remembered how waves of sexual energy washing through me were sacred.

Remembered it as if the memory were part of my body, in my blood, and in my cells.

I don't think it makes me special that I was able to have such a body memory of this ancient truth. I think the reason more people didn't remember this truth themselves, and don't remember it now, is because they've never been exposed to it—picked up a book or talked with or (bliss beyond bliss) made love with a person who might remind them.

❦

Reading Wilhelm Reich exposed me for the first time to the concept that sex was really about more than two bodies coming together. Sex was connected to the soul of a human being, part of our essence and our touchstone with the natural world.

Needless to say, I became interested in everything Wilhelm Reich wrote and became rather devoted to his brilliance.

Wilhelm Reich was not the first person to study the fact of orgasm, but he was the first person of the modern era to understand its significance and its necessity to mental health the way the ancients had. He was the first person to start a clinic devoted to sexual therapy. He was the first person to point out that people, even young people—even teenagers!—are naturally highly sexual beings, and to complain about "compulsory morality" that didn't allow us to experience fully or freely our own sexuality. He was the first to synthesize the work of sexual researchers and biologists, psychologists and physiologists, historians and sociologists, and theorize that repressed sexuality led to problems not only for the individual who could not access sexual pleasure, but also for the culture as a whole in which those individuals lived.

Disdain for our human sexuality was disdain for our own core—it was like trying to run a machine from which had been pulled the central pin that keeps all the other gears and cogs moving in harmony. The machine without its central pin broke down and couldn't produce; we humans, without a deeply felt connection to our central longing for love, were also broken down. We were broken down so that we abused our children, neglected our elderly, and broke each other's hearts with impunity. We raped and robbed each other, and went to war.

Reich was a great influence on a whole generation of therapists who still rely, and expand upon, his theories today.

For his stunning and yet entirely sensible approach to sex, Reich was booted out of Austria (under Hitler), and then he was booted out of England, and then he was imprisoned in the United States. His books were burned, and he died behind bars.

Such is, often, the end of visionary genius in our blind, bewildered world.

Once, sometime in the 1950s, when the book burning was at its height and the government bonfires were blazing out of control, I found a copy of Reich's work, *Listen, Little Man,* in a library. I wondered if it was one of the few copies of Reich's work still in existence and worried that it too would soon be found hiding there on the shelf, and destroyed.

My first instinct was to steal the book, in order to save it. I thought that I should preserve it in my own growing and eclectic library. But then I thought, no. There was a chance that the book wouldn't be destroyed if I left it in the library's care, but by stealing it I would make it unavailable to anyone else who might discover it on this shelf and become enlightened through reading it.

What I did was to check the book out, go home, and retype the whole thing, with several carbon copies to boot, so that, if, after I returned it to the library, it was destroyed, at least Reich's text would be preserved.

That was how devoted I became to Reich's genius.

I am sorry to say that it took me so long to act on my reaction to discovering Reich to find a way to spread Reich's words and to find a way to help enable people to embrace and celebrate their own sexuality.

I guess there were some personal things I had to reconcile before the concept of assisting others in this sort of adventure could occur to me. Notably I had to overcome my own resistance to pleasure and, in particular, sexual pleasure.

Look, I liked sex. In spite of my horrible initiation to it by that comedian when I was eighteen, I thought sex was a wonderful thing.

In general.

There were certain parts of it I didn't like.

I didn't really like intercourse itself, the part that Reich had termed "the Genital Embrace." Oh, with the right person, under the right conditions, it could be engaging, but I resented a little bit that I couldn't really participate in intercourse; men seemed to like it best when you were just lying there on your back, receiving them. I didn't like that sense of power of a man over me, and I really didn't like a man sweating over me, propped up on his elbows, thrusting away, eyes closed, as if he was alone in the endeavor, getting off without any regard for my presence, let alone my pleasure.

But I didn't know that sex—intercourse—could be any different. Like the vast (if not utter), majority of women, I learned about sex from men, from their point of view, the way they liked it. There were no books for young women that explained how to enhance our pleasure. Apart from medical texts, there were no books at all that explained anything about sex. Moreover, Freud still held sway—a woman's attachment to her clitoris was infantile. I thought the proper way—the only way—to have sex was to have it the way a man wanted me to.

The idea that a woman's freedom to express and enjoy her sexuality was integral to a woman's liberation would not have occurred to me then.

In fact, the idea that, by 1949, we women weren't as liberated as we ever were going to get would not have occurred to me.

I subscribed to the school of thought that stated that women had the vote, so we were now fully vested with all of our rights and responsibilities as citizens. Alice Paul, that fearless young woman who had been so integrally responsible for the passage of women's suffrage, had done it all.

And, those things that Alice Paul hadn't done? Well, it was a man's world. Men ruled the place, and I was just another woman thinking along these sad but standard lines.

I didn't even realize how sad this line of thought was—how depressing it should have been to know that no matter how hard you worked or how good you got, because you were born a woman, you were always going to come in second place, always going to get paid less, have less opportunity and autonomy, always have less of everything.

It didn't dawn on me then that perhaps that was why a woman like Eleanor Roosevelt had captured the imagination of so many women and won their admiration—she was a woman who was standing up, talking out loud, and making her own place in the world even though it was her very own husband who very much ruled the world in which we all lived.

※

My political energy, at the midpoint of the twentieth century, was directed not toward attaining women's liberation, but toward defending the rights of a group of men.

This was the time of the McCarthy hearings, the witch hunts of the House Un-American Activities Committee, and the plight of those whose patriotism was falsely, and sometimes fatally, attacked moved me deeply.

The House Un-American Activities Committee charged that Communists had established a significant base in the dominant medium of mass culture. Communists, it was said, were planting subversive messages in Hollywood films shown at home and negative messages about the United Stated in films that had international distribution. Of course, the hysterics completely ignored the realities —that evidence of leftist messages in the actual films was so slim that attorneys for HUAC at one point had to resort to citing as Communist propaganda the fact that the Russia children portrayed in the 1944 film, *Song of Russia,* were *smiling.*

Alvah Bessie, Herbert Biberman, Lester Cole, Edward Dmytryk, Ring Lardner, Jr., John Howard Lawson, Albert Maltz, Samuel Ornitz, Adrian Scott, and Dalton Trumbo were accused of being Communists. They were the Hollywood Ten. Prominent writers and directors and producers all, they were among the giants whose careers were derailed or destroyed by such nonsense. I volunteered to go to work for the committee that was trying to keep those men from being sentenced to jail.

Given that, during my upbringing, I had been very much encouraged to give of my free time to worthy causes, maybe it seems natural that I would be interested in helping save such important people from such outrage. Or, maybe, though the activities of the House Un-American Activities Committee have been thoroughly discredited in our time, I was always a little bit of a radical, even in my youth; but let me tell you, these were frightening times. Books were being burned. You got all of your Marx off your shelves and out of your house in case you were searched. You were careful what you said, and to whom you said it.

The appeals made to the courts on behalf of the Hollywood Ten were all denied, and they all served prison terms of up to one year.

The pervasive fear that settled over the Hollywood entertainment community when these convictions were upheld was one of the reasons I started to think about leaving Los Angeles and moving home to New York.

When some friends told me about an available ride back east with a fellow who wanted to travel there too, and I then also got word that my mother wasn't well, I knew it was time to go home.

The trip back to New York was a real adventure.

The driver my friends had found for me turned out to be both rather incompetent and unstable. It became my job to push and pull and pinch and prattle and prevent him from falling asleep at the wheel. But when I offered to take over for him in the driver's seat, he absolutely wouldn't hear of it.

For so very many reasons, it was such a relief to arrive back in Manhattan.

Chapter Eight

The U.N., the IUD, and the FBI

I came back to New York in 1951 with a few theatrical credits to add to my resume, several really well-done sketches of myself that the art students I'd posed for had gifted to me, a letter of glowing reference from Norman Corwin, and a personal library that had grown so large it made my friends joke that I'd better settle down soon because they didn't want to have to move it again.

I was twenty-nine years old.

Nearly thirty!

From the perspective of my eighties, I know, of course, how very young thirty is, but back then the looming birthday triggered, if not a crisis, a very thoughtful re-evaluation. I wanted a steady job, with a steady paycheck coming in every week. I wanted to help my brother, who was finding success as an interior designer, with our parents—I wanted to be responsible about that familial obligation. Mom's health issues, which had been part of my reasons for returning east, had proved not to be serious, but she and my father had settled together into the slow decline that would last for almost twenty-five more years—a decline I always thought was exacerbated by their dissatisfaction with each other, their unhappy couplehood.

And, hey, speaking of couplehood, I was twenty-nine years

old! If I wanted a husband and children, wasn't I overdue to get married myself?

The letter of recommendation from Norman Corwin helped me land a job at the United Nations. I had requested an assignment to the Public Relations Department—thinking that was where the skills I had honed in the Army could best be put to use—but the only job opening available to women when I applied was in the typing pool.

Still, I wanted the job they offered to me, and the steady paycheck that came with it. I turned in the formidable amount of paperwork the Personnel Department required of a new hire—including the "Loyalty Oath" that was a staple of McCarthy-era, government-affiliated employment, even at an international organization like the U.N.—and reported for my first day at my new office. It turned out that the work I was assigned was fascinating, and I liked the atmosphere too, the hectic pace of accomplishing work of international importance.

One of the most exciting parts of my job at the U.N. was when the General Assembly met. The verbatim reporters would record the speeches on their steno machines, and then they would come into the great big room that adjoined the General Assembly hall and dictate their notes to us typists so we could get them on paper for distribution to the world—the delegates themselves, the heads of nations, and the press. *Clickety, clickety, clickety*—the typewriters in that room went so fast and steadily that it was like we were staging a world-class tap dance revue. Politics had, you know, always held a great interest for me, and I was a voracious reader. I loved being in the center of the action like this, processing orations of global impact into the written word.

I had a bit of a crush on one of those verbatim reporters—Bernie—and he did ask me out on a date. I found out that he was married, though. I guess, from my experience with Bob, I just assumed that anyone who initiated an extramarital affair was unhappy in (or at least confused about) his choice of mate, but when I confronted Bernie and told him that he'd have to leave his wife if he wanted to pursue a relationship with me, he told me that although he cared for me deeply he had no intention of leaving his wife.

Like George, but without the joie de vivre.

I continued to date, but not frequently—and not Bernie.

I suppose I was on a search for my future husband though the idea of marriage, to me, was not a personal goal, only something that shifted around in the back of my mind like some inevitability. It was just something that would eventually happen to me, as it happened to everyone else. I enjoyed, in the course of the search, a good bit of sexual activity. After reading *The Function of the Orgasm,* I was probably more open and attuned to the body's need for sexual expression than someone who hadn't been exposed to Reich's theories; still, no matter the way the picture of a 1950s career gal has been painted in the media, enjoying a good bit of sexual activity wasn't unusual for any of us.

The big fear we all had at the time was getting pregnant. Birth control was a huge issue. It was hard to find a doctor who would provide birth control devices to an unmarried woman, although I continued to be able to find doctors who would fit me for a cervical cap when I needed a new one. These caps were hard to come by—they were manufactured in Europe and not readily available in the United States—but they were among the most reliable methods of the day and worth the effort it took to get hold of one.

A condom, of course, would have been as effective a method then as it is now, but I can't recall that any man I had sex with wore a condom, except maybe rarely. Anyway, I certainly would have been embarrassed to interrupt some great romantic event by asking someone to put on a rubber before we had intercourse.

Making sure that you didn't become pregnant was, at the time, strictly a woman's responsibility. No one thought of the issue as political; it was simply a thing women were expected to do in our culture, protect ourselves, not make our partner think about the consequences of the actions we were participating in together or hamper his pleasure in the act by requiring him to wear a device that might dull the sensations he enjoyed. Women got cervical caps or diaphragms, as later we got an IUD or a prescription for the pill, and we got on with it.

I got on with it.

I held a responsible job that I found very exciting, but I still wanted to keep my hand in acting. I dated with the vague notion of someday "settling down," but my focus was still on the stage. I wanted to continue to study and improve my craft, and I wanted to do it at the prestigious Paul Mann School of Acting.

Paul Mann was a maverick in a time of change—the McCarthy hearings segueing into the civil rights movement—his school was the first to integrate black and white students, and it produced, among its glittering alumni, Lloyd Richards (the first African American to direct a Broadway show), Sidney Poitier (who starred in Lloyd Richards's *A Raisin in the Sun*), Godfrey Cambridge, Ossie Davis, and Ruby Dee.

It was a struggle for me financially to attend Paul Mann's school. When I won a place there I thanked Paul profusely, though I told him I didn't know how I was going to be able to handle the tuition. The G.I. Bill wouldn't cover the tuition at Paul Mann's— perhaps because he was such a civil rights radical and on the blacklist himself. After my first year at the school I told Paul I just couldn't afford to attend any longer. In response, Paul said he needed a registrar, and he hired me for the job. For the next three years I got acting lessons and he got, in exchange, a damn good office manager.

I was blessed with a group of good friends—a lot of whom I'd known from before I'd gone to Los Angeles, and some of whom were new—and we spent most of our summer weekends together on Ocean Beach, at Fire Island.

I've always been a beach sort of a girl. The warmth of the sand and the sound of the waves can always relax me. Just getting on the ferry on a Friday night, after a busy week, leaving the city and knowing that I am going to a place where there are no cars and the process of unwinding can begin, was relaxing in itself.

The atmosphere on Ocean Beach was festive on these weekends. There was always dancing, and there were interesting people to talk to, and young men to go out with. I recall one particular party when a friend of mine who was a TV producer invited Buddy Hackett, who I thought was just a lovable fellow, and Carl Reiner, who I thought was just devastatingly charming. I got to talking with them at the party, and one of the other men in this group was so funny, another comedian, but this one just made me laugh until I cried for mercy. I was delighted when he asked me out on a date. We did go out but, I regret to say now, only once; I think Mel Brooks found me somewhat captivating, but I thought he was just nuts.

Some nights my friend Gigi and I would take a beach taxi down to the Pines section of Fire Island. The Pines was then, as it is now, a predominantly gay enclave, and we thought the parties the gay men threw were even more fun than the ones on Ocean Beach.

I got on with it—life—and I was making a very good one for myself.

Then, one day, at the U.N., after I'd been working there for about a year and had just earned a promotion out of the typing pool and into the Bureau for Eastern Affairs, a letter from the FBI came, addressed to me.

When I'd begun my job at the U.N., I was asked to sign that

Loyalty Oath. By signing it I swore, truthfully, that I was a patriotic citizen of the United States. I swore, as well, that I was not a member of the Communist Party, and that I never had been.

That last part wasn't the truth, but I rationalized it at the time by telling myself that I had joined the party when I was very young, long ago, and I hadn't been a member for even a year.

The letter that came to me that day from the FBI indicated when and where I was to have a hearing concerning my activities on behalf of the Communist Party.

I made an appointment to see a civil rights attorney immediately.

The attorney I contacted told me that if records did exist from the meetings of the Communist Party I had attended over a decade before and indicated that I had been a member of the party, combined with my more recent work with the committee to save the Hollywood Ten (though this work hadn't involved any formal party membership at all), it would be enough to convict me of perjury. I could be sentenced to time in jail. He recommended that I resign my job.

And, so, I left the U.N., but not without regrets. When was I ever going to get that close to being at the center of world affairs again?

Shortly after I resigned from the U.N., two FBI agents showed up at my apartment to question me about my "involvement" with the Hollywood Ten. The stereotype of FBI agents is of gruff and humorless big fellows in trench coats, and these two were that stereotype exactly. I remember thinking, Hey! I was just a little worker bee for that committee out in Los Angeles. All I did was stuff envelopes and count up names on petitions. I never got to meet even one of those ten great men who I was trying to keep out of prison. What do these big scary guys in trench coats want with *me*?

Shouldn't they have bigger—and *realer*—bad guys to go look up?

Then, as spontaneously as I had ever done anything, I gave the acting performance of my lifetime. I became, immediately and completely, a different person—I did a Judy Holliday impression that would have won me an Academy Award if anyone with a sense of humor had been there to see it. "Oh! What an *exciting* place that was to be, you know," I chirped. "That office where we did all that work for all those Hollywood people who were being sent off to prison? It was so glamorous! I don't know what the people were being sent off to prison for, but that office where we all met to help keep them out was just packed with men. I heard from a girlfriend, she said it was a really swell place to pick up a new boyfriend or two, and boy was it!"

The agents bought the whole act, and the FBI left me alone after that, but I can just imagine the information they might have collected over the years of my life—from activist for the Hollywood Ten to the owner of a sex toy store. If there's a dossier on me, I like to think it's a pretty interesting read!

Chapter Nine

Revelation
in a Bakery Truck

There is a newspaper photograph I have, black-and-white and yellowed with age. It is of a slender woman in her early thirties, a full-length shot of her taken at rather close range. She is wearing a good-looking trench coat and her hair, which is long and wavy, is well cut and attractively styled. The photograph shows her in mid-stride on a film noir night, her eyes narrowed with wariness. She is about to enter a police station.

The lessons we are given to learn in life are sometimes ignored—outright—or maybe only missed in the headiness of a particular time, a cultural phenomenon like the postwar boom, or one's own youth.

The caption under that newspaper photograph does not say the young woman pictured has just started a new job that she's very good at, or that she is a graduate of Paul Mann's Actor's Workshop, or that she has a new boyfriend who she is just really falling hard for. It says that she is on her way to city detectives at the local precinct to give her statement concerning her recent abduction.

My new job was at a small advertising agency, The Michael Newmark Agency, which specialized in placing real estate ads. My job was to assist the account executives in Mr. Newmark's office by writing the ads for the firm's existing clients and placing them in the newspapers. It was basically a one-woman show, after Mr. Newmark or another account executive had landed the account, but I have always been what you could reasonably call a workaholic. I put in such long hours and lavished such care and attention on the details of my duties that there were people who asked, even after I had been with the agency for only a short time, if I were one of its owners.

I was also in the midst of what I would have, at the time, called one of the great romances of my life. His name was Gerry Freeman and he was a reporter for the *New York Mirror*. I'd met him in the course of the contact I had with the city's newspapers for my new job, and what Gerry had to recommend him was intelligence, a frenetic sort of energy that I found very appealing, and a gigantic sense of humor. Gerry was still another case of my falling hard for a guy who could make me laugh.

I wasn't pursuing my aspirations to be an actress. There was a bit of an unwritten rule about Paul Mann not liking it when his students aggressively pursued acting jobs before we'd graduated and were grounded in our craft. I'd graduated, but I was caught up in my new responsibilities at the advertising agency and in my relationship with Gerry. I didn't possess the burning need to be on the stage, which would have kept me going through the hard work and rounds of rejections that were auditions.

One night, a dear friend of mine, Natalie, who'd arrived for a visit from Los Angeles with her husband and child, asked me if I would baby-sit so she and her husband could go out to attend the theater. I welcomed the opportunity to spend time with the baby and to spend some quiet time catching up on my reading after the baby went to sleep for the night. It was the uneventful evening I had hoped for myself, a nice break in my hectic schedule, until Natalie and her husband came back from the theater and I left to return to my own home.

My friends were staying in an apartment on the Upper West

Side of Manhattan, and I lived on the East Side at the time. The hour was late, and I was tired and anxious to get back to my apartment. My route home was fairly direct—the Eighty-sixth Street crosstown bus—and I stood on the corner to catch it. I had been waiting quite a while for a bus to come when a bakery truck pulled up in front of me and stopped at a red light.

While I had lived in California, hitching rides was a major form of transportation for those of us without cars in the sprawling city of Los Angeles. I, rather instinctively, stuck out my thumb at the idling bakery truck. "Would you like a ride?" the truck driver leaned over to the passenger window to ask me. "*Hop in!*" He said he'd take me along if I wanted to go across town because he was headed that way anyway.

I remember that I laughed—it struck me that, of course, I was in New York again, where people didn't generally hitchhike, but I still didn't think of this truck driver's offer as all that odd. He was just a kid, cute, with tousled red hair, ready to do me a favor.

I stood next to the door of the bakery truck and waited while the driver slid it open, and then I got in. There was no passenger seat in the truck, just open space filled with bread racks, so I braced myself with one hand on the dashboard for the drive.

As soon as the truck started to move east across Eighty-sixth Street, I heard a noise and turned to see a second man in the truck, standing behind me. He was drinking a beer. I couldn't see him very clearly in the shadows of the bread racks.

My guard went up immediately, as it will when a new piece of information is suddenly thrown into an unusual situation, but I wasn't distressingly uncomfortable—after all, this was a *bakery truck*.

Then the second man reached over from where he was standing and lightly—too lightly, and silently—stroked the back of my hair.

I froze.

I thought that pretending I hadn't noticed the touch was a good strategy, so I didn't say a word. Besides, at this point we were only midway through Central Park. Between two bad situations—being stuck in this sinister bakery truck or being stuck alone after dark in the middle of the park—I decided to stay with the one I was already in.

But I desperately wanted out of that truck, and when we were finally across the park I found my voice and said so.

"You can just drop me here," I turned and said to the driver.

"Aww," he replied, "I can take you the whole way home."

I was growing increasingly frightened as we continued to ride, but I held onto the thought that the driver looked like such a good, cute kid, and he did keep assuring me that he was going to drop me off right in front of my apartment building.

I reached toward the passenger door as soon as we neared my building, and the kid slowed the truck, reached across me, and started, to my great relief, to help me slide the door back. I began to get out of the truck even before it had come to a complete stop, but the second man called out from the back of the truck, as I was exiting the passenger side. Would I like to go out on a date with him sometime? I called back an emphatic, no, thank you, I was already dating someone else, and then I ran into the vestibule of my building. The second man was out of the truck, right behind me, grabbing at me, and before I could even begin to defend myself, he got his hands around my neck and started to choke me.

I remember thinking, in the split second I felt the pressure of his thumbs against my throat, that this would be such a stupid way to die.

Perhaps it was the realization that my situation was that dire—he had his hands closed tightly around my throat, and they hurt me so much, and I was sucking for air; I could really *die* here—that gave me the presence of mind to drop my purse, and the strength to fight him and accurately land that one blow or kick or bite, or whatever it was, that finally allowed me to break free and run.

I ran into the street, screaming. I heard the bakery truck screech from the curb. I saw a couple who'd been walking down the street come running toward me. I remember a police car pulling up, and my trying my best to tell the two cops what had happened.

"Did he take anything?" one of the cops asked me.

It was such an absurd question. I had just been choked so thoroughly that I was still coughing, still gasping to breathe properly, but the cop wanted to know if *he took anything*? If he took something, would that make what had just happened to me a crime?

The question was so crazy that it shocked me out of my panic. I realized that my pants were wet—that sometime while I was being choked I had wet myself. I was humiliated to be standing there in wet pants, and I realized, yes, he had taken something. My purse—my little clutch that I had dropped in order to be able to defend myself against my attacker—was gone.

I told the cops that my purse was missing, and that's when they got in the squad car and took off in the direction I had told them the bakery truck had been going when it pulled out.

Son of a bitch!

Clearly it wasn't an assault on a young woman but only theft that was the real issue here.

I went upstairs, to my apartment. I changed into clean, dry clothes. I told my roommate what had happened and, just that quickly, the police telephoned, to tell me they had found the bakery truck and apprehended the two men. They wanted me to go down to the station house to identify the thieves and make my statement.

I hesitated. I had certainly gotten a clean enough look at

both the men inside the bakery truck to make identifications. But what if both of them were just young kids, like the driver? What if it all had been a lark, a prank that got out of hand when I showed my real fear by jumping out of that moving vehicle and refusing so rudely the second man's request for a date? What if this was all my fault for being stupid and trusting and naïve enough to get in that truck in the first place?

Though it was the middle of the night, my roommate insisted on calling a friend of hers who was a lawyer, and she made me tell him what had just happened to me. "You should go down to that station house and prosecute those men," the lawyer said. "They're harming people."

I realized he was right; I had to report these two guys before they did the same thing to another woman.

The police came to pick me up and take me to the station house in a squad car. When we got there, there were newspaper photographers lined up all around the entrance, and it was me they were waiting there to photograph. These were reporters covering their beat, and I just happened to be the news that night. Flashbulbs started popping at me like I was a star at a cinema premiere.

Inside the police station, I found out that the two men I'd ridden with in the bakery truck didn't work for the bakery at all. They had stolen the truck, and the man who had choked me was fresh out of prison, on parole. The police were very forthcoming and overtly solicitous as they took my statement, but I was in a panic to get back home.

I felt like an idiot for having accepted the ride in that bakery truck. Moreover, no matter how I had insisted that I hadn't known either of those two men before I got into the truck with them, there was some question about my own complicity in the crime, and the police were not wondering about my smarts for having put myself in such a dangerous position. They were wondering about my morals. Only a "loose woman" would get into a truck late at night with two men she didn't know; maybe only a woman who was, in reality, a *prostitute* would do something like that.

I was desperately apprehensive that any of the pictures that had been taken of me at the station house entrance would appear in the newspapers. What if people assumed that since I was hitching a ride at two A.M. I must be a prostitute looking for business?

I got home and dialed the telephone wildly. I called up Gerry, my boyfriend, who was working the graveyard shift that night in *The New York Mirror*'s newsroom. Please call all your friends in the newsrooms at the papers and tell them not to print any of those photographs, I pleaded with him. Tell them I'm your girlfriend. Tell them I was just trying to get home from a baby-sitting job and I should have waited for the goddamn crosstown bus!

I'd like to think that it was an indication of the times that I was so frantically concerned, in the wake of my assault, for my own reputation—and that times have changed. I'd like to think young women today aren't conditioned to so quickly condemn themselves.

Sure enough, the next morning, there were photographs splashed all over the newspapers of me arriving at the station house. There was a big one in *The New York Mirror*, the paper that Gerry worked for.

The man who'd choked me was sent back to jail.

The attorney for the kid who'd been driving the truck came to me to go over my testimony. The kid hadn't bothered me, had he? If I would say the kid hadn't bothered me, things would go easier for him, and this was, after all, his first offense.

Gerry? Shortly thereafter, he up and married some other girl.

Chapter Ten

A Prescription

It was a revelation: you can't trust everybody. You've got to keep your guard up. You've got to be careful about what you do as a woman in this culture. Certainly hitching a ride in the city of New York was not appropriate; but there was more to it than that.

My sense of empathy was, as I have already stated, overdeveloped. Generally, the ability to identify with another person's suffering is considered to be a good quality—for me, it is what made me a good friend, an effective political activist, and it is why I am able to be so enthralled and moved by a painting hanging in a museum, or a piece of music. Hand-in-hand, however, with the facility for understanding the difficulties of another as my own came the willingness to trust them, to forgive, and to love.

And how could I really know who to trust, to forgive, and to love, when I could not extend the benevolence to myself?

It was the mid 1950s, I was in my thirties, and the revelation was crushing: I was reluctant to judge anyone else, but I could sure put myself on the rack.

There was no question that I was functioning to the full extent of my considerable capacity at my job. I was working hard, and well. The Michael Newmark Agency was prospering, and I didn't flinch about accepting the credit Michael gave me for that. Then Michael merged with two other men, Sid Posner and Pierce Mitchell, to form Newmark, Posner & Mitchell. I followed Michael to his new business, and the men were all grateful to have an employee who was so competent and dedicated.

During the week, at work, I was a dynamo.

On the weekends, however, I began to get headaches—migraines—just debilitating pain.

The headaches hit me when I got to Fire Island for the weekend, the place that had always been my respite, or they hit me as I was getting ready to go to Fire Island. I would be so sick with them that I couldn't get to the beach at all.

The headaches were excruciating ordeals. One Friday night, when the headache just wouldn't allow me to make the trip out to the island, I drew myself a hot bath and crawled into the tub, hoping to relax myself enough to dull the pain. As I lay in the tub I thought to myself how easy it would be to just let myself slip under water and drown—and the pain would be gone forever.

That's how bad the headaches hurt.

In the next moment, however, I thought, "I can't slip under water! That would get my hair all wet and I've just shampooed!"

It was such a ridiculous juxtaposition—don't drown yourself because you'll dampen your hairdo—that it made me laugh. Laughing made me feel a spark again, in the midst of my real agony, of how very much I loved my life.

When I finally confessed to one of my bosses, Pierce Mitchell, that I was now spending my weekends locked in my apartment with a monster, writhing in its grip, and I was going to have to take some time off to seek medical help, he told me about a man named Dr. Alexander Lowen.

Dr. Lowen, who was born in New York City in 1910, was a Reichian analyst. He was a man with both a powerful, eclectic intellect and a strong need for athletic activity. From the beginning of his professional journey he had been interested in the connection between mental and physical health. He had been attracted to Wilhelm Reich's theory of the mind-body connection and, beyond this theory, the development of bioenergetic analysis. Bioenergetic analysis is a therapeutic approach that combines work with the mind and the body to help people resolve their emotional conflicts. Dr. Lowen had sought out Reich himself in order to be trained to do this work.

I was eager to begin therapy with a doctor who embraced the theories that I had found, a few years earlier, to be so practical and inspirational.

One of the premises of bioenergetic analysis is that traumatic experience is held not only in the mind but also in the muscles of the body, creating chronic muscular tension, or, as Reich called it, "body armor." The role of the armor is to defend and protect its wearer from future emotional assaults. The bodywork of bioenergetics, which includes both specially designed exercises and hands-on manipulation, helps people to identify with their body tensions and release them through physical movement.

With Dr. Lowen, I worked primarily with a therapeutic tool called the bioenergetic stool. This stool is about hip high and the top of it resembles a small gymnastics horse, curved and comfortably padded. Dr Lowen would have me bend backward over this stool and hang there with the bones and muscles in my chest expanded, and, while hanging in such a position as long as I could take it, he would give me breathing instructions. After several minutes he would tell me to rise and to assume, on a mat on the floor, a position that is known in yoga as "Child's Pose."

In Child's Pose, my armor temporarily broken down by the breathing and stretching on the stool, I would cry.

And cry, and cry.

At first, *cry* was all I did. It seemed anything—any topic I happened to be thinking about—brought on tears.

Bioenergetic therapy harmonizes this sort of bodywork with a standard verbal analytic component to bring about intense identification of the source of psychic pain. Dr. Lowen began to help me to verbalize my pain as "an old longing," an old longing to be touched, and accepted, to trust and to forgive, and to love and to be loved.

At one point, on one Friday night shortly after I'd begun work with Dr. Lowen, I was unable to leave my apartment. I felt the pain and sickness of one of the headaches creeping into me and I realized that what was also creeping into me was a tremendous sense of sadness. I happened to look at myself in the mirror and I could see this sense of sadness in my face. It was not just an expression either, an arrangement of features that you would associate with someone who was sorrowful. It was as if my face were deflating, as if the sadness were a thing locked up in my body, sucking the skin against the bone, flattening the bone.

As soon as I acknowledged the sadness—in that *instant*—the headache lifted.

It was not difficult to understand that, at its most acute, this sadness—this longing—was for my mother, her touch, and her acceptance.

I could not say that my mother *withheld* those things from me, but that, from the time of "the Crash," she lost her ability to provide them. I could not say that she was neglectful of my welfare *materially*—my brother and I talked together into our seventies and rather marveled that, even at the Depression's worst, our mother managed to keep us fed—only that her need to have the fulfillment of these material duties acknowledged was physically and psychically exhausting. Mom's mantra since the Crash had been, "See? See how I sacrifice myself for you? See what I give up so you and your brother will have enough?" Now, in her slow decline, whenever I visited her, it seemed that it had become her duty to remind me, in those same blunt sorts of words, "I sacrificed my whole life for you and your brother."

Mom had given up her own needs, her energies, and her youth, so that Lorenz and I would be fed and clothed and schooled, and she bitterly wanted something back for that.

But in what form is such payment to be made?

Wilhelm Reich wrote: "People who are brought up with a negative attitude toward life and sex acquire a pleasure anxiety, which is physiologically anchored in chronic muscle spasms."

Dr. Lowen explained to me that my migraines were a manifestation of pleasure anxiety. I got the headaches from experiencing, or simply anticipating, the pleasures that my weekends at the beach held for me. It was too much pleasure for me to take. I wasn't worth it. How could I *spend* pleasure on myself when I had such an overwhelming debt of it to my mother?

At the end of three months of therapy, my headaches were gone completely, and I never had a migraine after that, though I continued in Reichian therapy for three years.

In this time I learned to express anger, which had always been a difficult thing for me to do. Even as a kid, if another kid hit me, I wouldn't hit back. Part of this passive acceptance was to doubt that I somehow hadn't deserved the blow, and an unwillingness to risk offense, and further loss of favor, by striking back.

Part of it was empathy, that I simply could not bear to see another person in pain.

In therapy I learned how to get mad—and I learned that getting mad was a healthy thing to do, and that there were reasonable ways to express the emotion.

I used to leave my sessions with Dr. Lowen feeling as if I'd had an orgasm because the process released, so intensely, the tensions I held in my body.

In therapy, I also began to understand my own powerful sexual energy as part of the condition of being human. Maybe, however—just maybe—my desire for a sexual partner was really a desire to be touched and accepted by another person. Was I searching out sex—even a sometimes substandard variety of it—when what I longed for was connection? Was I substituting penetration for closeness, and the subsequent, if temporary, relief of the ache inside of me?

I realized, in therapy, that it was possible to have sex without that old feeling of resentment. I needn't feel that my partner was somehow taking power over me, possession of me, needn't feel the humiliation of required submission overshadowing the act. I learned in therapy that this was, in fact, the way that sex was supposed to be: resentment-free, but I did not know how to achieve it.

I had another boyfriend at the time—David Meischonz, who was a few years younger than I was, such a sweet man, mild-mannered and good to me—and that relationship also petered out. I began to wonder if I was capable of loving someone, of giving my heart. I hadn't grown up knowing what the feeling of love could be and I didn't know how to identify it.

It was so terribly confusing.

Was my inability to identify love the reason that dear David had distanced himself from me? Had I hurt him, and shot myself in the foot in the process, by taking for granted a thing that was momentous because I was incapable of recognizing a great love when it was right in front of me?

I did know, however, that, sexually, I was able to love myself.

I knew I could have orgasms on my own. I could count on that, and this gave me a real sense of my own power. I didn't have to rely on someone else to take care of this basic need, so I could take my time looking and waiting for someone I *wanted*.

Dr. Lowen went on to co-create the Institute for Bioenergetic Analysis, in 1956. My regard for his mentor, Wilhelm Reich, has never waned. Myself, I worry that what I have just written here sounds too neat—that I haven't done justice to Reich's theories and Dr. Lowen's work and the impact they have had on how I have been able to live my life. It is, of course, a modern analytic cliché for a child to blame a parent for the lack in her life.

I bring up, again, the fact of my age. It is a mighty lesson for a child to take in at her mother's knee, that life is a thing to be feared and endured, not a thing from which to take joy and seek abundance. At 82, I still struggle with this thing I have learned from my mother; that's how mighty and crippling want of mother-love can be.

It's a funny—maybe even a shocking—thing to say: the founder of Eve's Garden struggles with pleasure?

Yes.

I embrace the concept of it, and I have spent the past thirty years of my life professing its goodness and rightness, and yet I still wrestle with my own worthiness of it.

I have significant regrets about the things I have and have not been able to accomplish. Whether I would or would not have had a successful career on the stage, for example, is something I don't know because I never even really pursued one—even as a graduate of such a prestigious school as the Paul Mann School of Acting, I was never able to accept that my talents might make me worthy of such a career.

I doubt not the worth of what I have chosen as my life's work, to sow the seeds of pleasure, but that I have done *enough* work—reached enough women and men with my message, touched enough people with the truth of it, operated my business and organized my life as if I were worthy of success and, in doing so, been as effective a messenger as I could have been.

Honesty compels me to write these things—honesty and an optimism that, in my darkest moments, is never completely absent.

Reich wrote: "The essential requirement to cure psychic disturbances is the reestablishment of the natural capacity for love."

How do we reestablish this capacity except by cultivating it in our children from their first moments on this earth with us?

My prescription: anyone who is reading this who is a parent—or a grandparent, or a godparent, or an aunt or uncle or some other figure of authority in a child's life—put this book down and go right now to that child. Pick her up from her crib, or wrap your arms around him, or dial your telephone and interrupt her in the middle of that meeting at her office, and tell her how very proud and lucky you are that she is your child. Tell her how much you love her. Tell him that the sun in your world rises and sets upon his happiness. Take him out to see a movie. Take her out to a ballgame. Sit down and really listen to music together—*his* music—and try to understand what he hears in it that touches him. Read a book or have a cup of tea or fold the laundry or wash the car together. Don't be afraid to lavish time and attention on the child; no one else will if you don't; you won't spoil her. Make it a point to reach out in some way every day to one of the children whom you love.

Like Reich, I believe that "the expansive process of biological pleasure is the productive life process per se." It is people who are most loved who have the greatest capacity for pleasure and for play, who are most able to love in return and to empathize with another, who can engage in their work not out of compulsive duty but a human's natural ability to derive satisfaction from creative and productive undertakings, who can internalize morality and not have need to impose repressive external restrictions and controls on how other people take their pleasure, who are both most curious about life, and most responsible about the freedoms they enjoy in it, because their freedom is founded in consciousness and based on knowledge.

It is parents who have the opportunity—no, the joyful *duty*—to create such whole, fully engaged individuals to people our society.

I have been blessed with many children in my life, particularly Gigi, Eve, and Cliffie, the children of my dear friend Stephanie Moro, who honored me by making me their godmother. Though I regret, as I have already said, never having become a biological parent, I think in the most vital ways I would have made a damn good one.

Chapter Eleven

At Last,
and Briefly

In the early 1960s I acquired two things I had been longing for, an acting career and a marriage. Both were blazing, dazzling affairs, and both were brief.

Ted Willms was good-looking, quiet, sweet, and artistic, a photographer whose work I thought was brilliant and which I respected enormously. We related to each other in bed beautifully— sex was playful and our connection profound, though he was fifteen years younger than I was. When we married I eagerly left my job at the advertising agency and threw my energies into helping Ted get established in what I was sure was going to be a smashing career in photography.

I found space and helped Ted set up a photography studio. I spent my days on the telephone, acting as his agent. If I'd gotten him an assignment, I spent my time in the studio working beside him as his assistant. I took great satisfaction in the domestic chores that made our sunny one-bedroom apartment on Lexington Avenue into a home. We tried, because I was soon to be forty years old, to get me pregnant. We entertained, frequently.

One evening we were entertaining a group of Ted's friends when one of them started talking about a film on which he was working. It was a short subject being produced by Hayward Anderson, titled *The Cliff Dwellers*, the story of a lonely Texan who couldn't get a date in New York City. An actor named James Hampton, a handsome and slyly witty young man who was later to become best known as Trooper Dobbs in the television series *F-Troop,* had the lead male role. I wondered out loud if Ted's friend thought there might be a part in the film for me.

There was—the part of a middle-aged woman who lived alone, worked as a waitress, and found the idea of this young man calling her up for a date so ridiculous that she ended up in a fit of hysterical laughter; the comic relief.

One of the things the role called for me to do was to laugh manically, on cue; to go from stone cold sobriety into a convulsive fit of mirth, on a dime.

I had been trained as an actress by Paul Mann, and I was deeply steeped in "The Method," an approach to acting that called for immersion in the part you were playing, the internalization of character and motivation. I had no idea of how to laugh on cue.

I called up a friend of mine, a fellow I knew who was a director, and asked him for a little coaching with this problem. He told me to simply pull in my gut and let go with great big belly-busting guffaws. I wasn't to worry about motivation, only about having enough air in my belly to expel effectively.

When I tried this on the set the next day, the resulting laugh infected everyone. The rest of the cast, and the whole crew, started to laugh along with me, and none of us could get ourselves to stop. Unfortunately, the scene that called for the laugh was one of the first takes we did in the morning, and none of us really got ourselves back under full control for the rest of the day.

It was delicious!

I was working the telephone to help create a career for a man in whose work I believed. This man, my husband, and I were making a home together and, every night, we were trying to make a baby.

And, suddenly, I was getting up in the morning to go to a movie set to film my very own featured part.

Let me pause here a moment, in the good times.

It was possibly because, each month, there was fresh evidence of our failure to get me pregnant that I started to find the marriage hard going.

Or, it could have been hard going because Ted didn't seem to be working as wholeheartedly at promoting his career as I was, or as hard as I had expected him to.

I began to give Ted assignments, little things around the house and the studio for which he was to be responsible. I felt no resentment toward Ted in our bedroom—he was a thoughtful and creative lover and he had helped me to get past that part of sex that I hadn't liked—but I did resent it when I asked him to take care of paying our monthly bills and then the bill collectors started calling. My sense of financial security has its roots in all those times we were dispossessed when I was a kid, and it can be fragile. My body, like a machine that had stripped some central gear, shut down to Ted.

"Why do I always have to take care of you, Ted?" I agonized, but silently, internally. Outwardly, I was collected and I moved us out of our place on Lexington Avenue into cheaper quarters on Fifty-seventh Street very near, coincidentally, to where Eve's Garden now is located.

In the dead calm in which I facilitated our move, I became aware that what was happening, maybe, was that I was expecting too much of my new, young husband. I was in my late thirties, ready to be married to a successful man and start my family; Ted was in his early twenties and perhaps not yet hungry enough for success. Perhaps he was overwhelmed at the thought of becoming a father. Perhaps he was even intimidated by a wife who saw something she wanted—like that part in *The Cliff Dwellers*—and went out and got it for herself.

I decided that if I wanted my marriage to work, what I had to do was back off and give Ted a little room and time to grow into the place where I was already. And I told him so.

Ted's response was to laugh, pat me on the head, and walk away.

Pat. Me. On. The. Head.

My fucking eye *pat me on the head*; who did that condescending little twerp think he'd married, anyway?

In 1962, *The Cliff Dwellers* was nominated for an Academy Award in the category of Best Short Subject, Live Action. And I was granted the annulment from Ted for which I'd filed.

I asked for an annulment because it was an easier way to go than a divorce. Ted agreed to it and we decided between us to give as the grounds for our annulment Ted's dislike for children, and his unwillingness to father mine.

A few years later, Ted remarried. The woman he married came with five kids.

Chapter Twelve

Alice

It was winter when Ted and I broke up, and I just wanted to get away from the city for a while. *North*, I thought, would be a terrific destination; I could do a little skiing.

The scenery in New England is so placidly lovely, the cold so bracing, the countryside covered in snow so quiet. It is, all of it, so healing; this is why, I believe, the prints of Currier and Ives remain popular—the world blanketed in white is a peaceful place, slowed down and still and, in the external stillness, your internal self can be expansive. I needed time to think, after leaving Ted, and the beauty of Vermont coupled with the vigorous activity of skiing would be my therapy.

I love to ski. Let me tell you how I learned to do it.

My old boyfriend, David, had introduced me to the sport. He arranged for us to go on a weekend bus trip with a company that not only took you to the slopes, but also provided lessons once you got there. The people on the bus, all of us, were beginners. I took to skiing immediately and, at the end of two days, when a prize was given to the "most outstanding student," I won.

Shortly after my first skiing experience, I arranged to take myself on a two-week vacation to Canada to pursue my new interest. At the resort, I signed up for further instruction, but at the intermediate level, figuring the "most outstanding student" would qualify for this advanced group. The instructor watched me ski just once downhill and sent me back to the beginner level class—apparently the instructors at this prestigious ski school in Canada, Grey Rocks, had higher standards than the ones who'd judged me in the Poconos.

After the two weeks in Canada I was still a beginner as far as Grey Rocks was concerned, but I was hooked. I wanted to ski every weekend and to keep on taking lessons to improve my skills, but on my small salary I couldn't afford to go as often as I would have liked. So I found a resort that needed a beginner's instructor and convinced them to put me on their staff.

I recall many of my students praising me for being a terrific teacher—I also recall how I avoided my students when I went on my own runs and my own more advanced lessons so they wouldn't see me "ski plowing," a very basic, low-level form for a new skier to get herself down the hill!

It was audacious to have called myself an instructor at my level of expertise, but gradually I got what I wanted, which was to be a very, very good skier.

⁂

That winter that Ted and I broke up, I asked around and was introduced to a nice young couple who owned a guest lodge in Vermont. They were looking for a desk clerk and were willing to give room, board, and a season's ski pass to someone who would take the job. I accepted their offer and became a ski bum.

My first order of business, the first thing I needed to think through when I got to Vermont, was what I was going to call myself now that I was no longer a married woman. I had taken Ted's name for my own—it was much more customary to do so then than it is now, and, frankly, I hadn't given a moment's thought to the idea that I wouldn't be known by my husband's name after our wedding.

My bosses at Newmark, Posner & Mitchell, who'd invited me to come back to work for them, were encouraging me to keep my new name. "Willms," they told me, was a more common, and therefore more memorable, name than "Zetlin." It would be easier on my clients.

I thought they were probably right and, still, the idea of keeping my ex-husband's name strained the thing inside of me that was trying to make sense of my brief attempt at matrimony.

One day the solution came to me. "Williams." *Williams*. It was close enough to "Willms" that it wouldn't be a difficult transition for anyone who'd known me by my married name, and it was even easier to remember than "Willms."

And it would be mine, a name I had chosen for myself.
Dell Williams.

Dell Williams, now officially forty and legally single, needed more than just her own name. She needed a full-time job; something steady, with benefits. She wasn't a kid anymore, and there wasn't anyone to look after her but herself. No more fooling around with the fantasy that she was going to get the break that would turn her into the next Ginger Rogers. No more young husband for whom to forge, out of her own strong will and tireless workaholism, a career as a photographer. No more waiting for the Next Big Thing.

These were scary thoughts, brutal and practical, the results of both an honest self-assessment and a crisis of self-esteem.

I had pretty much settled on the plan of accepting the offer to return to Newmark, Posner & Mitchell when, one day, I decided to take a couple of runs on some fresh powder before starting my shift at the lodge's front desk.

I have to say, it was like a scene from a movie. There I was, racing down the blinding white ski slope, the wind rushing at my face, and *The Hallelujah Chorus* thundering in my head like a score:

I could be an account executive.

I didn't have to work *for* an account executive; I could *be* one.

It hit me just that quickly and bluntly. I was in charge of the ads at Newmark, Posner & Mitchell anyway, all the media placement and all the creative work. If I was doing the work, then why did I think I needed to let a man put his name on it? The only thing I really wasn't doing was acquiring new accounts, and how hard could that be? You make a telephone call, set up an appointment, turn on the charm; if you had a good product—and I did have a good product; I was very, very good at what I did—what was so out of the ordinary that you needed a penis in order to accomplish it?

If I were an account executive, instead of earning just a small salary, 15 percent of the commissions on my ads would be mine.

The amount of money I could expect to take home every week would increase immediately. Moreover, I would be in charge of determining my income potential—it would be limited only by how hard I, myself, was willing to work.

I finished the season in Vermont—the couple that ran the lodge was depending on me, and I allowed myself the time as a well-earned vacation. When I got back to New York in the early spring I started to look for my new job as an account executive.

I picked up the *New York Times* and turned to the classi-fieds—the page with the listings for "Jobs–Male," because who would think to hire a *female* account executive? I circled a couple of the ads that looked promising and got one of the firms to actually interview me, a firm known as Commerce Advertising. I got that job.

I remember the first business lunch I ever hosted. My client ordered a margarita, and I didn't know if it would be some sort of breech of business etiquette not to have something to drink with him. I have never had a tolerance for alcohol—I am such a small person that even one drink is usually too much for me—but wasn't there some saying about it being impolite to let a man drink alone? I remember that I drank my margarita and then had to go to the Ladies' Room and sit until my head stopped spinning.

I remember that I was always conscious of having to have on a fashionable hat when I went to call on my clients. I thought that Bergdorf's had the best millinery department in town.

I remember thinking that I was making a *ton* of money—my weekly draw was a whopping $100, and the commissions I would get at the end of the year were adding up at such a rate that I found it almost unbelievable that such a fortune was coming due to me.

I remember riding the ferry out to Fire Island one Friday evening, seeing that whole, splendid beach laid out in front of me, and thinking that I would love to own a piece of it.

If it is difficult for any young woman out there reading this to believe that, at one time in the not so distant past, the Help Wanted classified ads were categorized by the sex of the employee one wanted to hire (or that it didn't take more than a little nerve to show up wearing a dress in an office that had advertised for a man), she ought to have gotten a load of how my knees started to shake at the revolutionary idea that I could buy a piece of real estate for myself.

For myself.

On Monday morning I went to my boss at Commerce Advertising and asked for an advance on the commissions that were due me at year-end. I wanted to put the advance down on the co-op I'd found for *myself* on Fire Island over the weekend.

I had to assure my boss that I didn't really want to wait until I found another husband before I considered buying property. I was sure I would be able to handle any electrical or plumbing problems that might arise all on my own. I had to explain to the mortgage officer at the bank all the reasons why a cute little thing like me was unmarried. I had to smile and bite my tongue bloody at the real estate agent's innuendos about a single girl living all alone every weekend, but I got my own little piece of beach.

True to form, I immediately got involved in good causes to the benefit of my new island home. I organized my neighbors in the planting of lush, ornamental grasses, and I was appointed head of the committee that was working to save the dunes from erosion.

Rather unlike myself (and I say this because I have been acquisitive about few things besides books all my life), I quickly became dissatisfied with the co-op. I wanted a house. As a young girl living in those furnished rooms with my mother and my brother, I had kept a little diary in which I had pasted pictures I'd cut out of magazines of houses. The houses I liked always had white picket fences around them, and little gardens where I could dig my hands into the earth and plant flowers, and maybe vegetables too, and watch them grow.

In two years time, nose to the office grindstone and a savvy investment strategy in place, I was able to realize my girlhood dream of having my own house and garden.

One other thing I did after I got my co-op on Fire Island—and this is an important thing—I got a cat.

She was a gorgeous cat. She had silky gray fur and expressive green eyes, and she was the smallest cat you ever saw. Held against my own small body, she seemed almost about the right size. She was smart as well, responsive not only to moods, as animals can be, but to words, as heedful as a dog. She was my dog-cat, and I debated for a long time about what her name would be. Then, one day, I saw her crouched down low, looking out my living room window, rapt, in wonder. Those big green eyes were in total thrall. Like Alice, in Wonderland, I thought.

"Alice," she became.

A person who isn't an animal lover is probably not going to understand the sort of connection Alice and I had. In fact, a person who hasn't ever had the advantage of even having a pet might think I'm a little off for what I'm about to write but, what the hell, it won't be the first or the last time someone misses a point I think is critical: I was completely in love with Alice.

Alice was a cuddler. When I got back to my home after a day at the office, all Alice wanted was for me to sit down and hold her and scratch her belly and let her roll around in my lap and purr. One day when Alice was upside down in my lap, it hit me: *this is what love is.*

This is the feeling you're supposed to have when you love a being truly and deeply and irreplaceably.

This *is* what I'd felt for Leonard.

And it was what I'd felt for David, too, however quickly my romance with him had petered out.

I get it. I understand. *I am able to give my heart.*

That night I spent in a great deal of reflection. I thought about Leonard, and David, and I mourned sorely that I had not learned before—*in time*—to recognize the love I had held for each of them for what it truly was. I spent a great deal of time, that night, in tears.

Later—*now*—I'm grateful for having identified the sensation of love at all, of course. I believe that I recognized it at just the time that it was right for me to do so. Certainly, for what was to come next in my life, I needed the capacity to turn my heart over and give it away.

Alice died on June 25, 1975.

I have been grateful every day since that she came into my life.

Gallery 1

My mother, Sarah Bronstein, in Paris around 1916.

Mom, with her sister Dora on her left, Paris, 1916.

My father, Isaac Zetlin, in Paris around 1914. He is dressed for a performance in the chorus of the opera company with whom he sang.

My parents' engagement photograph. Mom was about seventeen, and Dad was about twenty-four, though I think be looks so very much younger than she does.

This is my mother's family, on the eve of my parents' engagement.
Dad is standing to Mom's left; he designed the flowered dress she's wearing.
Mom's got her arm around her beloved brother, Simon.

Dad, speed skating in winter . . .   . . . and bicycling in summer.

Mom, with two of the cups she won on the tennis courts.

Young bathing beauty Dell, summer of 1924.

Sarah, Lorenz, and Dell Zetlin, winter 1926. The shadow in the foreground is Dad, I've always thought that this photo explained eloquently the place he would make for himself in our lives.

Dell and Lorenz Zetlin together on the beach, summer 1927.

Dell, Isaac, and Lorenz Zetlin, spring 1929.

Lorenz, Sarah, and Dell Zetlin, summer 1929, just months before "The Crash."

Sarah, Lorenz, Isaac, and Dell Zetlin, summer 1929,
in a rare photograph of all four of us together.

My high school graduation portrait, 1940.

With Bebe and Annette, on the beach, summer 1941;
that's me on the right.

Up a tree, 1940; left to right are Joyce, me, and Bella.

Dell, Sarah, and Lorenz Zetlin, spring 1941.
I love this photograph because it's the only one I have in which Mom is smiling.

One of my publicity shots taken for my acting portfolio, 1941.

Formal portrait Mom had taken just before I joined the Army, 1941.

Part Two

Awakening

Chapter Thirteen

The Goddess Calls

I can't say that I believe in fate, but I do believe that nothing happens accidentally. There are forces in the universe that put things in your path. If you pay attention, remain curious and alert, there are unexpected opportunities all along the way. I believe this because throughout my life, every time I've thought I've reached a peak, I've come to find out it was only a plateau.

In 1970 I was forty-eight years old, and the view from the peak I thought I was living on was magnificent.

I'd left Commerce Advertising sometime in the mid-1960s when one of the men who worked there with me left to start his own agency and tried to take my business with him. The client list I'd built up over the years was impressive, and the commissions I generated from it were the envy of the office. This man went behind my back to acquire my list. It was a professional upheaval the likes of which changed forever what I understood about how business could be conducted, sneaky and mean. I survived it by telling the clients who he was trying to steal exactly what was going on—by being honest with them. I moved to another agency, Miller Advertising, with my client list intact. A year or so later I was wooed by yet another firm, Bernard Hodes Advertising, and I was able to bring all of my clients with me when I made this move.

In short, I had a large and loyal client base, and all of my energies were devoted to servicing it and making it grow. I had found my life's work, I was good at it, and it supported me in style. I had a weekend house on my beloved Fire Island and all the hats from Bergdorf's I could want.

A great friend of mine, Stephanie Moro, who goes back with me all the way to our days together at Paul Mann's, said something recently about this time of my life. I feel as if it's a little self-aggrandizing to report her words to you, but they really do sum up the sheen that was on my life at the time: "We all looked up to Dell. She was our American success story. She was the Big Mama."

It was from this peak, having the admiration of my friends and looking through an office window overlooking Fifth Avenue in New York City, that I gazed out upon the world.

One day in August of 1970, I happened to glance out my office window and take in the view. One of the copywriters at the Hodes Agency was standing beside me, and his eyes followed mine, glancing out too.

These weren't exactly idle glances—we'd heard there was going to be a big parade that day, and no one could help peeking out the window every once in a while to see the preparation for it on the street below.

What the copywriter and I saw outside, on Fifth Avenue, were women gathering in preparation for marching up the avenue. It was the first Women's March for Equality, and the crowds it was attracting, activists and onlookers, were huge—5,000 participants alone as it would turn out.

"Look at all of them," I said, softly. What I was feeling was a sort of *awe*, I suppose, a wonder that so many women would come together on a hot summer day to draw attention to political issues that were important to them. *Women's issues*; issues that impacted on the way women were able to live their lives.

Though my understanding of those issues was peripheral—

information I'd read about in the mainstream press which, therefore, was meager—I felt for the first time moved by the sheer number of women out there on the street to consider that the issues on parade were, indeed, *our* issues.

Mine.

But, of course, that was just a ridiculous thought! I saw myself as a woman who had made it in the world. I didn't need to be liberated, I *was* liberated: I was at the top of a tough profession in the greatest, most unforgiving city in the world. I owned a home of my own. I dated whom I liked and when I wanted to—what need did I have for a bunch of malcontents? And what was I doing looking out the window anyway when there were projects on my desk that needed my attention?

"Yeah," the copywriter returned with me to the work at hand, and he scoffed, "Guess they don't have anything better to do."

The copywriter was a young man whose work I respected and whom, by extension, I had also respected personally; one who, I'd supposed, had given me respect in return. But suddenly I wasn't so sure about that, about how he felt about me.

In what sort of esteem could he hold me when he could dismiss so offhandedly so many others of my kind?

Was I just the house broad then? The career gal making good in a man's world and not making a fuss about who really ran the place? Playing by the rules, careful not to overstep, eager to blend in, the token girl, the token Jew, the token black, *the good nigger*? Yoko Ono phrased it just so astutely, that gut reaction I had in that moment that the copywriter scoffed: Woman was the nigger of the world.

The body produces chemicals that create natural euphoria. "*I* have nothing better to do today," I said to the copywriter, and my body kicked in to overtime assembly line mass production of those chemicals. "I think I'll go down and join them."

I left my office and went to stand with the women in the park. At first I wasn't at all comfortable—these were women with an agenda and, attracted as I was to the idea of it, I had no real concept of their collective politics. But I met them and talked with them, and I exchanged stories with them as we milled about, waiting to set off. When the crowd began to move, I marched with them.

I wish I could organize into a neat package of words the thoughts that went through my mind as I worked my way along Fifth Avenue, one among thousands that day, chanting beneath unfurled banners and waving placards, clutching hands, and clenching fists.

I could say that my consciousness was instantly raised, but that wouldn't begin to describe the sort of a high I was on.

I could say that all of the experiences of all my life came together in one split second on that brilliant afternoon—all of the sexual put-ons and political slights, the sly pas de deux I'd had to perform with bosses and bankers and boyfriends for what suddenly seemed endless, aching eons—but Jane O'Reilly[10] has already described that *click* moment so well, the instant the bulb finally goes on and the light's almost too bright for you to stand.

I could say that the march was a transformational experience but that phrase too is now overworked and feels inadequate to convey the sense of pride I felt that day in being a woman—how this pride was not at all an intellectual experience but one that affected my bones and my muscles and my cells.

And my soul.

If, on the day of that march, I made reference to any deity, it would most certainly still have been a paternal one, but I knew immediately that I had been called by some power greater than my

---

[10] Jane O'Reilly, "Click! The Housewife's Moment of Truth," *Ms. Magazine*, 1972.

own, to some higher purpose.

I had no way of knowing immediately what the purpose was or the nature of the work that satisfying it would entail—that would take a few more years to become clear—but I understood even before the march had ended that my life's work was still undiscovered and ahead of me.

The copywriter who scoffed at me and got my feet moving down to the park that day must remain anonymous—I have no idea now what his name was—but I want to take this opportunity to thank him. The Goddess used him as her instrument, and he was a most effective messenger.

Chapter Fourteen

Bud Light Babe

In the early days of the modern women's movement, the late 1960s and early 1970s, much was made of names—the words we used to name ourselves, and the words that others used to name us. The word *woman* was seen to be imbued with more dignity and seriousness of purpose than other words—girls, gals, chicks, and birds—to which females were expected to respond.

In 1970, at the age of forty-eight, I became a *woman*. So profoundly did we need then to define ourselves, our dignity and seriousness of purpose, and so deeply was I impressed with this need, that I can still get angry with the wrong person coming up at the wrong time with the wrong term.

You should have heard me shouting at my television set in the spring of 2004 when Sofia Coppola was honored as the first American *girl* to win an Academy Award for Best Original Screenplay. In context it was all wrong. Here was a person who was clearly an adult receiving an award for doing quite a grown-up thing. How odd it would have sounded in our ears if Jack Nicholson had been presented as the first *boy* ever to win three acting Oscars!

Context is everything.

Immediately after the march up Fifth Avenue, I went to the table where volunteers from the National Organization for Women were recruiting new members and I signed up. A month later I was contacted, via mail, and went to the bustling midtown headquarters of the New York City chapter for my first meeting.

Jacqui Ceballos, a woman with such fighting spirit that I took to calling her "our fearless leader," was president of the chapter then, and Carol DeSarum was another of the chapter's s articulate and committed volunteers. I remain close to both of these dear women, but our friendship was able to take root in the first place because we worked so frequently side by side in those early days. My job as an account executive gave me the flexibility I needed to take an active role within the NOW organization. I was available to attend demonstrations and help organize. Eventually Jacqui, a good general who knew how to delegate, asked me to take over as chairwoman of the fund-raising committee.

I didn't know bubkes about fund-raising, but the post was vacant, and I had a habit of going ahead and doing a lot of things I didn't know how to do. "The Goddess may not always call the qualified, but she always qualifies the called," is my motto. Besides, those other things I'd gone ahead and done? Assisting Norman Corwin, and being an artist's model, and becoming a ski instructor and an account executive? They'd turned out all right—a little creativity, a little elbow grease; I could handle the challenge.

This is the way my mind works.

After I'd accepted the post, Jacqui showed me the books. It was clear that we needed to raise some working capital *fast*. I decided that celebrating something was the best way to do that. The fifth anniversary of NYNOW was coming up, and it seemed like a good excuse to me to throw a fund-raising anniversary celebration party.

I went to see Art D'Lugoff, the owner of the Village Gate. I knew Art from my younger days, haunting the music clubs downtown. He agreed to let me use his place for the party on a Sunday, a night when he was normally closed, and he would let NYNOW use it at no charge.

My committee sent out announcements about the party to the members of our chapter, and we sent press releases to the newspapers in hopes of attracting new faces to the event.

We invited Bella Abzug, Shirley Chisholm, Betty Friedan, Flo Kennedy, and Gloria Steinem to be guests of honor, and all of them accepted.

We got merchants to donate door prizes and coordinated a menu of hors d'oeuvres from the membership so that we wouldn't have the expense of a caterer.

Hundreds attended.

Between the price of admission and the sale of raffle tickets and the auctioning off of other prizes, we raised over fourteen hundred dollars for the chapter that night—a respectable sum of money now but a big deal back then.

It wasn't until the evening was over and the event a resounding hit that it even entered my mind it could have been anything but. I think this is one of the keys to success: sigh with relief, if you must, after the fact, but don't contemplate failure until you've pulled it off.

Instead, work hard, and cultivate chutzpah.

I had called up the fellas at that bastion of testosterone, Budweiser, and asked them to donate the beverages for NYNOW's Fifth Anniversary Gala. They did and, ever since, whenever I have a beer, it's got to be Bud Light. I'm very loyal. I'm—in context—a Bud Light Babe.

Chapter Fifteen

Feminists
Don't Like Sex

From the vantage earned over my thirty years spent in educating and encouraging women to reclaim and embrace our erotic autonomy, it is frustrating to have to acknowledge that this nasty rumor is still in circulation.

Feminists don't like sex? I still can't quite figure out how it got started.

Maybe it got started in the early days because some of us feminists like sex in ways that are different from the traditional, patriarchy-approved model.

Some women who are feminists like to have sex with other women, and maybe some people found the reality that all women don't like to have sex with men intimidating.

Maybe Jane O'Reilly[11] was right: "Women who assume authority are unnatural. Unnatural women are lesbians. Therefore all leaders of the women's movement were presumed to be lesbians."

Or, maybe, we feminists ourselves helped to foster a media image of ourselves as ball-busting, men haters with the bickering and bitching among our own constituencies that did go on in those early days. Lesbian Separatists had one idea of what the movement should be about, young mothers out in the suburbs had quite another, and,

---

[11] *The Girl I Left Behind*, Jane O'Reilly.

quite frankly, not many of us had a lot of time to recruit minority women or listen to their concerns.

No, I don't mean to make it sound as if women like Shirley Chisholm and Flo Kennedy didn't have quite a lot of important things to say—no one could marginalize those dynamos even if they tried; the truth is these women *were* the dynamos furthering our cause—I am only acknowledging that we were accused of being a middle-class, all-white organization; between the schisms within our own ranks and the myriad of critical issues that vied for and divided our attention, our concerns might not have been as inclusive as they could have been.

We fought among ourselves. Because dissension among human beings always gets better ratings than a dry statistical story, the press ate up our divisions. It was easier to label us all as lesbians—to use that label to marginalize all of us—than to present a well-thought-out analysis of the dry statistical facts.

Shame on them—and shame on us if we let them do it to us one more time, in the next go-round; but I'm getting ahead of myself again.

Maybe that nasty rumor about feminists being disinclined toward sex got started because some of us feminists like to have sex with several different men over the course of a lifetime rather than with just one approved specimen, and that was frightening for some people. They had to watch us as we emerged and put the lie to the fairy tale that a woman's sex drive was minimal and, anyway, tied more intimately to financial security than anything remotely feral, or fun.

They had to watch us gather together, talk to each other, discuss sex, and learn where our clitorises were; and they had to listen to us ask for *better* sex; that probably scared the hell out of some people.

Maybe it was the antipornography movement of the 1980s

that did it. Sexual violence against women was and remains an international crisis but, while the debate still rages about whether pornography exacerbates incidences of sexual violence, *nobody* ever said all sex was rape. Nobody ever tried to throw out the baby with that bath water; I'll never figure out how we let that one get away from us.

The risk of unwanted pregnancy and the exhausting debate over choice, the rise in the rate of occurrence of sexually transmitted diseases (STDs) and the tragedy of the AIDS epidemic, priests molesting little kids and ten year olds giving each other blow jobs—sometimes even *I* don't like sex so much; I have to remind myself that it is sexuality perverted by patriarchy that has led to every one of those ills.

Personally, my first reaction to the rumor that feminists don't like sex is to laugh.

Follow me: people who identify themselves as feminist generally have better educations about the issues that affect women *and women's bodies* than the population as a whole. We, therefore, know women's bodies better and like sex *more* than the unenlightened Jane or Joe.

But the truth of the matter is probably that feminists like sex or don't like it any more or any less than any other segment of the population.

The fact of the matter is, however much we liked sex and with whom, sexual liberation has been a core issue of the modern women's movement from day one, an essential plank of the platform. Right up there with equal pay for equal work has been the goal of separating the function of sexual reproduction from the function of sexual pleasure.

As Rebecca Chalker puts it in her must-read book, *The Clitoral Truth*, "If we don't struggle to achieve equality in the sexual sphere, it is possible that achieving equity everywhere else will rest upon a shaky foundation. In other words, anatomy is not destiny so much as the social construction of anatomy is destiny."

In my words: The whole woman demands to be free, and our sexuality is an essential part of the whole.

Sexual liberation is a core issue of the women's movement that slips, often more and sometimes less, from the center probably because we live in a culture where grown-up people are so stunned by an open and rational discussion of sex that they either snicker or start moralizing. Keeping the issue at center is often either a battle with the prevailing political winds or a compromise with the concerns of special interests.

Except for a few outstanding anomalies ("How Your Love Life Keeps You Healthy," the cover story of the January 19, 2004 issue of *Time Magazine* comes to mind), the mainstream media itself is both far too titillated by and squeamish about the subject of sex to report on it with any sense of the holistic simplicity of the concept behind sexual liberation.

All right. How did I learn to speak frankly—openly and rationally—about sex?

I met Betty Dodson.

This meeting was in 1970. We met by chance, at a Yoga retreat weekend where we were assigned to bunk together in the same room. I immediately took to Betty—she is confident and honest and you feel safe around her. She is an artist, by training. Some of her art, at the time that we met, was being printed in a small alternative newspaper—OK, it was actually a ghastly porn paper—but the art was extraordinary: strong, beautiful bodies engaged in ecstatic sex, partnered and solo, and I admired it a great deal.

For all of my immediate attraction to Betty, however, I didn't call her for a long while after our workshop weekend. My excuse was that advertising was a seasonal business and I was swamped at the office.

The truth is that Betty was, also at that time, beginning to conduct her own workshops, in self-pleasuring—the ones that would help to liberate so very many women over the course of the next three decades. I was extremely intrigued by the premise of these workshops—that is, fostering a woman's appreciation for the beauty and strength and sexual potential of her own body, and how this appreciation is the basis upon which we build the self-esteem necessary to claiming other rights and freedoms. I knew that when I called on Betty I wanted to sign up to take her masturbation workshop, and I had to work up the nerve.

Took me months.

I arrived at Betty's house to begin her workshop feeling anxious and apprehensive. Her workshops are conducted completely in the nude—instructor and participants, all buck naked. I did not know how I was going to be able to strip down, appear before a group without my clothes, and do Goddess knew what else. I did not know how I was going to be able to go through with this. I stood outside of Betty's apartment door and had to talk myself into ringing the bell.

Betty answered my ring. She opened the door with a big smile and drew me inside with a big hug. She did this while she was not wearing a stitch.

For an instant this pride and easiness with her body was shocking to me. I mean, for heaven's sake, I was the type who was still wearing fashionable hats on a daily basis! But in the next instant Betty's nakedness was a source of power—a radiance emanating from all of the confidence and honesty that had been so initially appealing to me—and I couldn't wait to shed my own trappings, skirt and blouse and hat and inhibitions, and tap into that source.

Betty ushered our group of naked women—there were about a dozen of us—into a large room she'd created especially for these workshops. The room was empty of furniture, but it was done in soft colors, softly lit, and it was deliciously warm, and there was thick carpeting on the floor. We sat on the floor, on big, cushiony blue pillows, in a circle. The circle is an important symbol in the ancient Goddess worshipping religions; the configuration fitted Betty's workshop to a tee. Not only did it facilitate ease of discussion and demonstration, it made all of us an equal part of a never-ending group dynamic energy.

Betty began the workshop by leading us in a discussion about our bodies, and the images we ourselves had of them. It was a lively talk; the body types represented in that room ran the gamut. We were athletically muscled and we were painfully scrawny. We were short and slender and we were tall and clinically obese. We were young and angular and we were rounded from pregnancy and birth. We were ripely bosomed and we were flat as a board and we were sagging with age. The thing that still stands out for me about that discussion is that every one of us had mostly negative things to say about the bodies we lived in. Even the couple of women in the group who fit the standard definition of *knockout* were critical of themselves.

It was depressing to hear how awkward we all felt in our skins, and it was inspiring to sit there with Betty, in the presence of someone who clearly took such glory in her own middle-aged body. Betty was beautiful, and she knew it; how come this was so hard for the rest of us?

The second thing Betty had us do was play show-and-tell.

One by one, Betty had us open our legs. She placed a mirror

on the floor before our vulvas and we looked at them. We looked at our own vulvas, and we looked at each other's vulvas. Betty told us to use both of our hands—not just a timid few fingers—to open the outer lips of our vulvas so we could really *look*.

While we looked, Betty lovingly named each part of our vulvas for us, so we would all know what those parts were really called. She made one woman gasp with appreciation at the rich chocolate-purple of her outer lips. She arranged with care and an artist's eye the butterfly wings of another's inner lips. She helped one woman coax the shy button of her clitoris out of its hood.

I had never looked at my own vulva before this. I had not looked at anyone else's either. I had certainly never expected that if I had looked at one it would be spellbinding. But it was. All of them were. They were marvelous things, complex and mysterious, accessible works of art we lived with every day. If only we'd known!

Betty taught us the common names for the different parts of our vulvas, and she urged us to see how uncommon and miraculous each of our individual vulvas was.

Everyone's was different!

This was revolutionary information.

Everyone's was different and everyone's was deeply beautiful, like every different snowflake that falls from the sky. I was suddenly so happy to have the one that was mine.

More than happy.

It was a part of me. It was a part of me I had neglected, or ignored, and, finding it now, I was 100% me. I was whole.

Women often cry at this point in Betty's workshops. They are tears of joy: I have found myself. I have come home.

On the second day of the workshop, Betty introduced the group to the Hitachi Magic Wand.

The Magic Wand was, and remains, the gold standard of sexual enhancement accessories. It has a long, light body and a round vibrating head about the size of a peach. The head, which vibrates with a frequency (intensity) controlled by its user, is placed upon the clitoris. The head can be placed directly on the clitoris, or to one side of it; often a soft bath cloth or napkin is placed between the vibrator's head and the woman's clitoris, particularly if the woman using it is not accustomed to such direct clitoral stimulation. The soft, consistent, steadfast vibrations of the Magic Wand produce—well, sheer ecstasy.

Betty used the Magic Wand to give us a demonstration of the techniques of masturbation. She turned on the vibrator and, slowly and sweetly, placed it on her clitoris and began to pleasure herself.

The group watched her, fascinated.

When she brought herself to orgasm, we broke out into applause.

Then Betty gave each of us a Magic Wand of our own so we could try out the techniques she'd shown to us. We formed a circle on the floor. We sat on our pillows or lay back on them. A few of us straddled our cushions. And then we began to pleasure ourselves.

Some of us were intimidated by the immediacy of the gratification the wand produced—and of our need to vocalize this—and we stifled ourselves.

"Don't be afraid of your voice," Betty said, touching her fingers to one woman's throat and allowing her to release the sounds of her pleasure.

Some of us were embarrassed about the intimacy with ourselves, and with our own desire, that masturbation called out of us.

"Try fondling your breasts at the same time," Betty encouraged another, and the woman responded eagerly to the suggestion.

Some of us felt self-absorbed, or maybe greedy is a better word, by how much we *wanted*—and by how much pleasure we were capable of.

"Don't stop yourself," Betty whispered when one of the women started to open her eyes, switch off her vibrator, and sit up after she'd had her first orgasm. "Keep going. Go again," Betty said.

I had certainly not shed my own inhibitions easily or immediately, but through the course of the two days of the workshop, in a conducive atmosphere created by a supportive teacher, I found myself less and less able to hold on to preconceived notions and conditioning. I found myself becoming attuned to my own core, my own power—the power that Betty seemed to so effortlessly possess—and to this same power in all the women in our group. It was not an intellectual communication, but something far more primal, and vital.

The energy raised by a group of women coming and coming and coming together . . . it's like, if someone lit a match, there would have been fire.

Chapter Sixteen

Miracle
on Thirty-fourth Street

There's a story about me that makes the rounds from time to time, and people who hear it wonder if it's true. I'll tell you now, it is.

The day after completing Betty Dodson's masturbation workshop, I took myself to Macy's to purchase my own Hitachi Magic Wand. It was a Monday. I was on my lunch hour. I was one year shy of my fiftieth birthday, a successful advertising executive, and I was dressed the part, in a well-cut suit and good shoes. I walked up to a pimply, twenty-something sales clerk and I asked him where the body massagers were located.

"Body massager" is what we called a vibrator in those days, in stores like Macy's, under the pretense that we were all taking them home to relieve the strain on sore shoulder muscles.

"What do you want it for?" the kid demanded, loudly enough that people turned to look at us.

If my clothing had disintegrated at that very moment, right there on the third floor of the department store, I couldn't have been more mortified.

I mumbled something about having a bad back.

The kid led me to a shelf near the back of the electronics department, where a Magic Wand was on display. It was plugged in, ready for demonstration.

My hands were shaking—the kid was watching my every move—but I picked the vibrator up as if it were nothing more than an electric razor, and I was being a smart consumer by doing some comparison shopping. I turned it on.

It had been set on "high."

Betty Dodson had recommended, in her workshop, that the Magic Wand be used on "low." I recommend now that it is used on "low," especially for women who are just beginning to experiment with this happy toy, but it can be used on "high"; it's not unheard of. Set on "low," the sound of the Wand's vibrations is gentle, soothing; set on "high" its sound is not really that much more noticeable, which you already know if you happen to own one of your own, so forgive me if this comes off as overreacting. It was 1971 and I was in the middle of a busy department store. The buzzing sound that Wand made when I turned it on seemed so loud I jumped and fairly threw the thing back on the shelf so that no one alerted by the noise would see me holding it, know what I was thinking of doing with it, and sneer.

A sense of guilt and shame made me want to run—gather up my red Spanish shawl and run off this stage and into the arms of some sympathetic teacher. Where was Betty Dodson when I really needed her?

But I am tenacious.

I knew that if I didn't get over my fear then and there and buy the Magic Wand I was never going to own one.

And I wanted very much to own one.

"I'll take it," I told the kid.

I left Macy's that day, clutching my precious, anonymous brown shopping bag and thinking: someone really ought to open up a store where a woman can buy one of these things without some kid asking her what she's going to do with it.

Chapter Seventeen

Knowing

Shortly after the incident at Macy's, late in the winter of 1973, the then-president of NYNOW, Judy Wenning, proposed that our chapter sponsor a Women's Sexuality Conference. Because promoting the basic core concept of sexual liberation had become a focus of mine, Judy asked me if I would help to organize the event.

Looking back at the poster Betty Dodson designed to advertise the conference (it is still framed over my desk), I am pleased and amazed at how ambitious we were. The conference was planned as a two-day event to be held that June, at a high school on Park Avenue and Ninety-fourth Street. We expected to attract a large audience and the conference was designed to consist of over thirty different workshops, most for women only. Some of the workshop titles were "Creating a New Sexual Identity," "The Right to Sexual Self-Determination," "Expanding Heterosexuality," "Older Women's Sexuality," "Teenage Sexuality," "Radicalizing Sex Education," "Racism & Sex," "Sex and the Handicapped," "Roles and Reversals," "Lesbian Nation," "Friendship, Trust & Sex," "The Double Standard," "Overcoming Inhibitions," and "Tantric Yoga and Sex," and that was just to start.

The workshops were comprised of women only because my conference co-creator, Laura Scharf, and I felt that this would create a more comfortable atmosphere in which the participant could be open and honest about her sexual issues.

Since men, however, have always been welcomed as members of NOW, we did set up a separate space for men who wanted to attend the conference, where they could meet and realize their own agenda. Warren Farrell, who since has authored several intriguing books—*The Myth of Male Power, Women Can't Hear What Men Don't Say,* and *Liberated Man,* to name only my personal favorites—organized and led the men's portion of this conference.

Over 1,400 women and men participated in the conference. The memory of the logistics required to coordinate space for all of those workshops, organize child care, contract for food service, and arrange for a band—a seven-piece all-women rock group called "The Dark Innocents"—to play at Saturday night's "Pleasure Party" can still make my temples throb.

The conference, overall, was a greater success than we had anticipated at our most hopeful, but two of the workshops stand out for me through time.

The first was called "Speak Out."

The idea of "Speak Out" was to simply gather women together in the auditorium of the school and let them speak for themselves. Let them give voice to the experience of their own sexuality, and their own experiences of sex.

Laura and I selected women with many different sexual histories and orientations to speak from the stage, as bearers of representative stories, one or more of which might touch one or more women in the audience. After the "Speak Out" presentation from the stage, we were scheduled to divide into smaller groups in which every woman in attendance who was inclined might have the opportunity to share her own private story.

Betty Dodson broke the ice by speaking first—about masturbation as a primary sexual lifestyle; it still amazes me to remember how many of those present sighed with relief at the validation of her own primary source of sexual satisfaction—but once the words began to flow they kept on coming, not like a tidal wave, but like an irresistible current.

Women spoke about loving their bodies, and hating their bodies. We heard stories about heterosexual sex and lesbian sex, bisexual sex and masturbation. First sex, and sex over sixty. Oral sex, and clitoral orgasms. Tender sex in committed, connected relationships, and wild, one-night stand sex, and lousy sex. Funny sex, and sad sex.

And incest and rape.

It was the first time that many of the women who spoke that day had ever told her story. In those days—the days when telling our stories to each other in consciousness-raising groups was vital so we could begin to know how common our stories were—it was the first time many of us had heard a narrative that came anywhere near to her own experience.

I mean, can you imagine the relief of becoming aware that you are not the only woman who does not come to orgasm through penetration alone? Of realizing you're not defective because you require more direct clitoral stimulation? Of thus finding the courage to ask for what you need?

Can you understand the horror of hearing how common the story of rape is in women's lives and the simultaneous connection with every other woman who has endured it? Survived it? How your shame in it, shared, is dissipated and, through speech, collectively transformed?

It was 1973; *it was the first time many of us had heard a narrative that came anywhere near to our own experience.*

The importance of the consciousness-raising groups of the 1960s and 1970s—where women gathered in twos and tens and more and began, for the first time in the modern era, to compare our stories and create a collective narrative for ourselves—cannot be overemphasized. An injustice perpetrated on an individual can't even be a personal tragedy if the victim isn't aware of the wrong done to her, but bring the victims together and watch them blossom with common indignation and strength, and suddenly you've got a movement.

I think it is an understatement to say that there wasn't a woman in the auditorium at the Speak Out who wasn't transfixed.

The other outstanding workshop of that conference weekend took place on the second day, a Sunday. It was a presentation of a slide show that Betty Dodson had created called "Creating a Female Genital Esthetic."[12]

Betty believed (and believes) that in order for a person to approach life with a sex-positive attitude, she first has to have a positive approach to her own body—she has to experience her own vulva as beautiful, as a work of art, and, in order to do that, she has to experience and appreciate the reality of the beauty of *all* vulvas.

As Betty was able to do for the few who were lucky enough to take her workshops, she wanted to do for the many by presenting a lovingly curated museum-style show of full-color, larger-than-life-sized slides of various vulvas, a parade of pussies—young pussies and old pussies, dark purple pussies and blush pink pussies, bushy pussies and bare pussies, pussies engorged and pussies in repose.

Betty's commentary, accompanying each slide, was at the same time light-hearted and impassioned, and always riveting. "Look!" she said, "Look at this gorgeous Baroque masterpiece! Notice the velvety burgundy color of it, and the deeply fluted inner lips. And, look at this

---

12 Betty Dodson's slide show is not, at this time, available either in print or for presentation. I recommend her book, *Sex for One*, for its stunning charcoal portraits of female genitalia, and also *Femalia*, by Joani Blank, which contains excellent full-color photographs, toward developing your own sense of awe and appreciation.

one! This is a classic Danish Modern model . . . "

The show was explosive. When it ended, when the last slide went to black and Betty stopped speaking, there was a brief, pregnant pause—millions of brain cells conditioned over millennia to feel shame for our female genitals were suddenly confronted with their intrinsic beauty; it took several seconds to know how to respond to the stirring of the ancient DNA where the memory of pride and strength and wholeness is stored—and then the auditorium exploded with applause and stomping feet and passionate cries—"Yes, yes! YES!"

I am aware that for some of you, reading these last few chapters has been a stroll down the memory lane of the movement. For others, it has been, perhaps, an exercise in astonishment—they didn't know about *that*?

For still too many, I fear, it may be an inventory of all that remains unknown.

Begin to know.

I implore you, *begin to know.*

The Monday after Betty made that slide show presentation, I went to work, as always. I passed the office of a fellow account executive on my way to my own office, as I always did. I heard that account executive belittling his secretary, as he frequently did. I stopped at his office door, as I never had before, and I said, "Where do you get the nerve to talk like that to another person?"

I say without qualification that I would never have had the pride or the strength to do that before Betty's presentation.

Knowledge is power.

If you do not know, begin.

Chapter Eighteen

Thanks, Henry

Before I became involved in the women's movement, I had looked upon lesbians as, er . . . well, different, as if some part of their psyche was not fully developed and that explained why their sexuality was not fully developed either.

I was also a little intimidated by lesbians back then. I thought of them as having some sort of inside information they weren't willing to share with me.

I had always admired women, the strength I saw in us, starting with my own mother, and I had been attracted to more than one or two women in my lifetime—remember one of my first crushes I told you about, chubby and magnetic Doris? And quiet, lovely Ginny?

Nevertheless, I believed that women loving women was not the natural order of things. It was not the way things were done.

I think I can be forgiven for this distortion of my view because I was conditioned, pretty much as all women were, to think of a man of my own as the ultimate attainment.

Henry Kissinger set me straight.

So to speak.

Kissinger's remark that "power is the ultimate aphrodisiac" got me thinking; and it cleared my vision.

If all a woman truly desired from a man was his power and, by association, some authority of her own in the world—and if I truly believed that women were equal to men, with equal authority—then (a two-tiered treat!), I didn't have to look to men to provide me with a respite in which I could enjoy respect: I could assume authority of my own, and be free to be attracted to, and to love, someone irrespective of their gender.

Elaine—just the thought of her makes me smile!—was one of the first women I invited into my life as a lover, and she was one of the great loves of my life. She was slender and athletic, with dark hair. I found her physically very attractive, but it was her down-to-earth quality that I fell in love with. She was highly intelligent too, really wise, and, the coup de grace, she could make me double over with laughter.

I distinctly remember thinking, during the time that I was falling for Elaine, that my love for her was a good thing, and a natural one, as if I were still talking myself around decades of a mindset that told me there was something innately suspect about homosexuality. But I also knew that our connection was nothing short of divine. The compatibility of woman-to-woman intimacy left me breathless. I thought there wasn't anyone else in the world who would be as perfect for me. I thought Elaine and I would be together all of our lives.

We had little more than a year, only two full summers, to spend together at my house on Fire Island.

Then Elaine was diagnosed with breast cancer.

She got so sick.

Today, because of early detection and advancements in medical treatments, many women survive the disease. I still wonder if Elaine's sickness were happening today maybe she would have survived it.

Not all of the time Elaine and I had together was an exercise in bliss. We had a relationship filled with the sort of ups and downs all couples experience—and some of the time it was rockier than that. I believe though, that had Elaine been given more time, we would have spent it together.

We would have had the rest of our lives together.

As it was, we had only the rest of Elaine's.

What I still have, however, is the memory of how Elaine and I laughed together when I told her how Henry Kissinger had cleared the way for me to fall in love with her.

To this day I cannot keep myself from having a good chuckle whenever I see Henry Kissinger going on about something on CNN. I cannot tell you the number of times I've had to explain to someone that it's not foreign policy that strikes me as so hilarious.

Chapter Nineteen

Another Word
About Marriage

Ambivalent.

I had passed the age, at this point, where bearing biological children was possible. The most basic, legal benefits I would need to derive from marriage—i.e., a support structure in which to raise my children and financial support for myself while I brought them up— were no longer a part of my thinking.

Moreover, because of my activities in the women's movement, my thinking was broader in general. Ted, my ex-husband, had had the nerve to pat me on the head as if I were a child when I had tried to discuss issues with him that were imperative to the strength of the sort of marriage I had longed to have. If my child-groom had the audacity to treat me with such disrespect, I could only imagine what life was like for the women who'd married within the more traditional age ratio.

The way that Ted had condescended to me had triggered the final collapse of any willingness I'd had to continue our union. Now, I began to question the *ownership* of woman by man that marriage, in our culture, seemed to imply. Was it this sense of his *ownership* of me that had provoked Ted's arrogance?

My discomfort with what the institutional concept of marriage implies in this country is a thing I have yet to resolve personally other than to know it is not an institution I want to enter again.

Love, however, is a thing about which I am not ambivalent at all.

When two people come together in love to support each other in sickness and in health, for richer or for poorer, in good times and in bad, that is marriage.

Who needs a piece of paper to declare it so?

The problem with my thinking is that declaring it so is, of course, the point.

The recognition of the community is a bulwark. The community before whom two people declare their intention to go through good times and bad ones together provides the social support and legal framework in which the new couple can progress more securely and more joyfully through their union.

From the benefits a child reaps when she grows up in an extended unit of family and friends, to health care benefits for a spouse who is staying at home or working only part time in order to devote the bulk of his energies to child rearing, to pension benefits paid to a surviving husband or wife, the community declares to the two people who come before them, the value of the marriage.

The problem with my thinking is that, too often, our community does not value marriage, but only the declaration of it.

Why else would we dance with abandon at a lavish spread thrown for a twenty-something bride and her young groom, but groan in disapproval when two lesbians who have been at each other's side for twenty years—in sickness and in health, for richer and for poorer, in good times and in bad—want to declare their commitment before our community?

George Bernard Shaw said, "All progress is initiated by challenging current conception, and executed by supplanting existing institutions."

Marriage, as I have said, is an institution about which I am wary. I believe it needs to be, if not supplanted, then redefined. Perhaps we can strengthen the institution of marriage—stem the rising divorce rate among those who actually do marry, and make marriage less politically unappealing to all of us old radicals—if we make it less about whatever sex the couple may or may not share and more about abiding love.

Chapter Twenty

Planting
the Garden

In four short years, from early 1970 until early 1974, I had awakened to so much. I had been exposed to so many great women with so many ideas that were as magnificent as they were, once uttered, utterly obvious: Women are people too. Fully people. We ought to be able to invest of ourselves in any endeavor we chose without feeling grateful to any man for allowing us the expenditure, without indeed feeling, as I myself once had, that we were blessed to be admitted into a sphere heretofore inhabited only by the male of the species, and that we were superior to all the women who were still left on the outside.

All of this fresh, life-giving, life-altering information had been laid in the soil at my feet. Seeds that I had been, at the outset, only curious enough to tend to had taken root and sprouted and now offered me jungle cool shade and heady fragrance and beauty so new and rare that it could hurt my eyes to look at it.

Strangely, though, this gorgeous place from which I could now look out upon the world offered me little peace. I couldn't live there all alone or only within the company of what was still such a small elite. The information that had been gifted to me demanded to be shared. Truly, I had an image of digging up one pretty flower at a time, potting it in its own pristine white ceramic pot, and presenting it to one woman at a time so she could place it on her desk at work or on her kitchen countertop, nurture it, and watch it grow into a dense, lusty jungle.

But what seed to plant? Where to start? How to begin when there was so much to be given away?

To me it was clear and vivid: among all of the issues that the women's movement had to address in order for my gender to achieve the freedoms so long withheld from us, the most vital was that we wrest control of our own bodies away from anyone but ourselves.

As long as anyone else could tell us what category of job we could or could not apply for, based on whether we had a vagina or a penis, we were not free. As long as there were schools that would not admit our brains because we brought our uteri along with them, we were not free. As long as we could not determine how our bodies were to be used to our own reproductive purposes, we were not free.

As long as one person's body is controlled by another, in any way, that person is a slave.

To me, liberation could come only through the rejection of any attempt to undermine the authority of a woman over her own body. It could come only through loving and knowing, respecting and revering, and reveling in our own sovereign sexuality.

I approached several women I knew who owned small retail businesses and asked them to start stocking the Hitachi Magic Wand; none of them felt the item was quite right for her inventory.

I had been approached by an entrepreneur who wanted to set up booths at NOW events to sell his own brand of vibrator. It was called the Prelude 3. It was small and white and came with a wealth of attachments including a divine little egg-shaped thing designed specifically for clitoral stimulation. It was an intriguing device, but it was not a Hitachi.

"Why don't you just do it yourself?" Betty Dodson asked me. "Open up a store and sell the Wands there?"

The image that flashed through my mind—movie buff that I have always been—was of Mickey Rooney turning to Judy Garland and enthusing, "Hey! Let's put on a show!"

I had absolutely zero experience in retail.

On the other hand, when had lack of experience ever stopped me before?

And I was looking desperately for any excuse to distract myself from my grief for Elaine.

And, in truth, I realized that the creation of a supportive and discreet means for a woman to purchase the tools of pleasure, and to learn how to use them, was important work that no one else seemed to be willing to take on. It was something I'd been toying with doing myself anyway. Betty's inspiration moved me to put my money where my mouth was.

I threw myself into the adventure of creating this means, and the venture became my new love.

I left my office at Hodes Advertising on the evening I decided I would call my business "Eve's Garden," and took myself out for a sushi dinner. (Raw fish, for some reason, always helps me concentrate.)

Over some really wonderful ahi tuna, I wrote the mission statement that you read at the beginning of this book. It came out of my pen as if it were being dictated by the Goddess herself. I have never again felt both as thoroughly passionate and as utterly calm as I did while my pen was moving across the paper that night.

But the *rightness* I felt as well on that night has never left me; I had found my life's work.

I knew, at last, the contribution I was supposed to make.

Through the growth of my business and the personal and

professional obstacles I faced (and, especially, the ones I did not overcome), the commitment I made has only expanded.

Eve's Garden opened for business in September of 1974; the rest is not yet herstory.

Gallery 2

Lorenz, in a publicity photo for the Bronx Variety Players. I love the way he inscribed it: "To my wonderful Sis, Your Loving Brother, Lorenz."

One of the photographs of Lorenz taken at the time of his screen test, the day before he shipped out to the Panama Canal.

United States Army Tec 4 Dell Zetlin.

Lorenz in the Army, performing his famous Carmen Miranda skit.

A sketch of me done by an art student, John Gregory,
when I was modeling at the Art Institute of California, 1949.

Photograph from *The New York Mirror* on the night I was abducted
in the bakery truck.

Outside of my apartment building in New York, fall 1956.

My husband, Ted Willms, a professional photographer,
took these photos of me in our home, 1961.
I love them because they show the character of Ted's work,
and for the playfulness in the two of me jousting with the fireplace poker.

Playing on the beach at Fire Island, 1965.

On the deck of my home on Fire Island, 1968.

Alice, 1969.

Playing the role of "Adam" in a Women's Rights demonstration at the
Atlas Statue in Rockefeller Center, 1973. (Photo: Bettye Lane.)

Demonstrating for Women's Rights, 1975. That's Jacquie Ceballos standing to my
left, between two unidentified protestors. Note my ever-present hat,
and the politically incorrect fur coat! (Photo: Bettye Lane)

Betty Dodson and me, Eve's Garden party, 1977. (Photo: Bettye Lane)

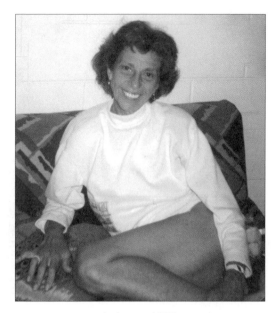

At home, 1978.

An Eve's Garden PR photo, 1979.

At home, with Honey, 1982.

Marcia Corbett, me, and Betty Dodson at Eve's Garden
Fifteenth Anniversary Party, 1989.

Playing on the beach in Hawaii on my seventieth birthday, 1992.

At home, 1994.
(Photo: Bettye Lane)

Rev. Dell Williams today.

Part Three

Teaching

Chapter Twenty-One

First Fruit

I am beautiful.
I am loveable.
I have a right to pleasure.
My Body Belongs to Me.
(But I share.)
Eve's Garden Affirmation

In September of 1974, when Eve's Garden opened for business, it was only a mail order concern. All of my customers were generated through a four-line advertisement in the classified section of *Ms. Magazine*—"Liberating vibrators and other pleasurable things for women from a feminist-owned business. Send 25 cents for our catalog. Eve's Garden, 119 W. 57th St., NYC."

It is not true that acceptance or not of my ad caused such a heated debate at *Ms. Magazine* that a meeting of the board of directors had to be called to settle on an outcome.

Look, I could write paragraphs of praise for Gloria Steinem, the magazine's founder, but what's important to say here is that though the magazine's major, mainstream advertisers frequently sent Gloria letters encouraging censorious reviews of her content, those letters never influenced the magazine's editorial policies. *Ms. Magazine* never refused an ad of mine. Upon occasion, Eve's Garden even received some editorial space of its own. Eve's Garden has always been the recipient of generous support from the magazine.

In September of 1974, the Eve's Garden catalog offered only three items for sale: the Hitachi Magic Wand, the Prelude 3, and Betty Dodson's book, *Liberating Masturbation*.[13] And Eve's Garden itself was my kitchen table.

When the orders poured in and started to overflow onto my stove and countertops, my brother saved me. Lorenz would meet me at my apartment at 5 P.M., after we'd both left our day jobs for the evening, and he'd help me pack and ship.

Many of the orders that came in, then as now, were accompanied by intimate and touching letters. I read them all and I have saved quite a few of them. Here are a few samples:

> So great to learn about you! God knows I've tried long enough to find a good, inexpensive vibrator— went through lots of J.C. Penney stores and catalogs and sales ignoramuses . . . .
> You may never know my agony.

> Which vibrator is really the best?
> I am a pretty open-minded but not too experienced 55-year-old divorcee . . . .

> Dear Eve's Garden,
> This is a love letter.
> I've just christened my new vibrator with my very first orgasm.
> Thank you.

Initially I thought your [promotion of vibrators was]

---

[13] Now in print as *Sex For One*, Betty Dodson; still a classic.

a bit commercial and even corny. I've now had mine for less than 24 hours and am writing to apologize for my judgmental thoughts and to thank you.

You are doing women a great service. Now I won't have to die wondering . . .

In September of 1974, vibrators were sold, in the main, in seedy porn shops, and they were of the cheap, plastic variety, not Hitachi's. To invest the Hitachi with the legitimacy it deserved, it was my inspiration to reach out to physicians and therapists, both on an individual basis and through umbrella organizations, to urge these professionals to attend to their patients' sexual health. I still have four giant, clunky, old-fashioned Rolodexes filled with hand-typed address cards of the doctors and psychologists who referred their clients to me. I kept, as well, the following letter from a woman in Austin, Texas:

Dear Ms. Williams,
I have never been in a—what should I call them?—
*"movie house"? "Porno shop"? There really isn't a
name, is there?*

Anyway, I've never ventured inside because they were always oriented toward men, and not the kind of men I would particularly care to have leering at me while I inspected vibrators!

Anyway, I saw your catalog in my doctor's office, of all places, and decided to send off for one. The whole idea of having a "garden" of goodies for women run by women appeals to me and eliminates my hesitation about dealing with you.

My husband laughs at me, but let him laugh!

I like to think that in September of 1974, I helped plant the tiny, transparent idea that our human sexuality is a divine gift, and letters like the two that follow give testimony to the fact that, even way back then, women were understanding this. We were getting it. The logic inherent in the ancient knowledge of healing sexuality was not escaping us.

> I was in the . . . ministry for many years.
> What you do is a ministry also, and you do it very well.

> May the great Goddess of the universe,
> our own earth, and all the heaven,
> bless Eve's Garden and everything in it.

The letters inspired me to branch out and advertise in other feminist publications. I was absolutely ravenous to reach as many women as I could, and I had to hire a third employee to handle all of the requests this additional exposure generated.

Under a year later, the volume of business that Eve's Garden was generating had grown to where I felt confident enough to resign from my job at Hodes Advertising. The Garden wasn't a gold mine, but I felt I would be able to live comfortably on the revenues. Besides, from its inception Eve's Garden had commanded my heart, and now it was demanding the bulk of my time as well.

I arranged a lump sum buyout of my accounts at Hodes and put the cash into the business. I rented an office on Fifty-seventh Street and moved the shipping operation out of my kitchen. I hired a bookkeeper—Ruth Libby, the same woman who I had called out that account executive for belittling. The *Village Voice* ran a story about the Garden. Though the *Voice* and *Ms.* were still the only two English language publications daring enough to give the concept of a woman's sex shop editorial coverage, I was starting to get a lot of European press. I decided to expand the business when the office next door became available. I rented it out for the shipping operation and turned the larger, existing space into a retail store. It was both ingenious and serendipitous: a shop in an office building, on an upper floor, where my customers could shop discreetly. I wouldn't allow men to come inside this space—not out of an overriding ball-busting, man-hating, feminazi philosophy, but to create an environment where women could be free to explore their sexuality in privacy, and safety.

I made the space elegant. Lorenz painted a large mural of a garden in it. I expanded the product line and staffed the store with trained employees, women who were both knowledgeable enough and sensitive enough to provide sound advice and guidance about issues of sexuality. I wrote some flyers, little how-to sheets, to accompany the products we sold. The space was big enough so we could gather women to consciousness-raising groups, and workshops like Betty Dodson's, right on the premises.

The showroom of Eve's Garden, when I got it opened, seemed to me to buzz with activity and energy from its first hours. Women found their way easily to what was intentionally a secret, but not secretive, place.

"I'm sixty years old," one of my first in-person customers announced. "I've been married for forty years and I have four children and I've never had an orgasm." She pounded my counter with her fist. "Give me whatever it is you've got."

"I don't know what to do with this," whispered the Orthodox Jewish woman, her beauty apparent but her own hair hidden under an expensive, mandatory wig. She unwrapped the Magic Wand she'd ordered from me through the mail. Shyly she explained that she didn't think the whole head of the Wand would fit inside of her. Softly, and confidently, I explained to her how the Wand was meant to be used. We spoke very quietly all the while that we talked—she was so apprehensive that her family would discover her purchase; it was as if our raised voices alone might alert them—but she left the Garden nodding her head, a smile on her face.

"Oh, my God!" The gasps that accompanied the discovery of mother by daughter shopping on the same day at Eve's Garden required even more diplomacy than I was used to dispensing. Confronting the sexuality of a different generation can be a startling experience in our culture, especially when those generations are so closely related, but this mother and daughter left Eve's Garden together that day, on their way to lunch and what I expect was an illuminating, and vastly comforting, discussion.

I was working seven days a week, and I loved every minute of it.

I loved writing clever copy for the catalog, finding new products to stock, and trying them out. I loved being in charge, too, making all of the decisions and knowing the buck stopped on my desktop. I loved that the business supporting me and so many staff was an extension of my commitment to the women's movement, an everyday ongoing demonstration of women empowered.

Eve's Garden did begin to offer workshops in our storefront space—notably the ones run by Betty Dodson that I had found so personally enriching—and I managed to attend other workshops and conferences regularly myself, to further my own education about sex, and to promote the Garden.

I didn't donate much of my time at all to NOW after Eve's Garden opened. What I was doing at the Garden I was doing as a feminist, and spreading the message of sexual liberation from my office on Fifty-seventh Street filled admirably both my time and my desire to make a contribution to the cause.

I began to be seen as a spokesperson for the cause of sexual liberation.

Eventually, I was given an offer to write a weekly column for a lesbian newspaper, *Sappho's Isle*. I was offered speaking engagements which I accepted gladly, the better to spread the good news (not to mention to be on stage and satisfy the life-long dream of an attentive audience—talk about a win-win situation!).

I got a few awards over the years. In 1977, the National Women's Health Coalition named me "Woman of the Year" for my contribution to women's sexual health. I was included in the 1988 edition of "Foremost Women of the Twentieth Century" and was listed in "Who's Who Worldwide," a registry of outstanding women business leaders (1994-1995). I was also listed in the first edition of the "International Who's Who in Sexology," and, in 1994, I received the Uncommon Woman award from the Uncommon Legacy Foundation.

I'll speak quite frankly, in this last section of this book, about the regrets I have in the ways I sometimes cultivated the Garden, but every piece of fruit that has sprouted there, from the early, heady days until now, has been sweet.

Chapter Twenty-Two

Brave
and Crazy

Frequently, when I talk to people about the work I have done through Eve's Garden, they refer to me as a "pioneer" and remark about how courageous I must have been to take such an edgy stand about a topic that was then so unexplored and controversial.

I am not going to shy away from any accolades on the subject. Yes, it did take nerve to do what I did.

When you denounce, within a patriarchal culture, what Rebecca Chalker calls "the theft of women's right to comprehend, define, explore, and experience sexual pleasure on our terms rather than through male standards," you are bound to make a few enemies. When your work further involves "salvaging masturbation from thousands of years of religious condemnation," it's much easier for some people to denounce your concepts as crazy than to try to break through the boundaries of their own inhibitions and ignorance.

I've been picketed (once by a group of men just longing to come inside the Garden), and I've received some hate mail. I've been the subject of personal attacks that were very hurtful. For example, because I have made public statements in support of the rights of sex workers, some people decided that, at some point, I had to have been a sex worker myself. My upbringing was such that this accusation offended me, initially, as one upon my honor. Now I am offended by its assumption that working as a prostitute isn't honorable. (You know, if you allow yourself, you grow.)

None of these attacks was devastating to me because that rightness I spoke of earlier, that clarity in knowing that my work was providing an essential service, let me find the calm in any storm that arose, and put any criticism in perspective—consider the source, and all that.

Also, although I took a strong and unconventional stand, I by no means stood alone.

My dear friend, Betty Dodson, was there at the forefront too. I like to think I caught her back and kept her going as often as she did for me but, as I said, Betty's the one with the unassailable confidence, and I think she probably did most of the catching.

There is Joani Blank who, about a year after I started Eve's Garden, opened Good Vibrations in San Francisco. Her pioneering work helped to expand our culture's understanding of the core ideals upon which we both built our businesses. We've been friendly competitors for going on thirty years, but every barrier one or the other of us has faced down has helped both of us.

There are close friends, like Lucille Bella, Jacqui Ceballos, Bettye Lane, and Stephanie Moro who, no matter how our focuses diverged, have long been there to support my professional commitments and to mother me when I needed that for more personal reasons.

Let me say a few words here, as well, about just what it is, at its most basic, that I've actually done.

My colleagues, Dr. Marty Klein and Dr. Alice Ladas, have both suggested that the real contribution I've made to the "sexual revolution" is, by being fairly average myself, to make an above-average sex life seem attainable for average people everywhere.

I like that.

I'm not (all of my early efforts at fame aside) a Hollywood star, and I don't surround myself with the trappings of glamour. I mean, for all of what is a real appreciation for fashion, the uniform I'm seen in most frequently is a pair of double-pleated slacks and a single-breasted blazer—and, more likely than not, they're both *beige*.

Though I'm at the vanguard of the sex toy industry (and for all of what has sometimes been flamboyant enthusiasm in the promotion of sexual freedom), I'm not flamboyant or "in your face" about my own sexual preferences. In all honesty, that's probably because my preferences actually wouldn't make for very wild copy but, more importantly, they have also been *perceived* as neither extreme nor excessive.

If, by presenting myself as a frankly sexual human being, in the context of all of the normality of that condition, I've been able to help raise the expectation of pleasure for others, what's really so radical?

What's not to like about that?

Personally, what I really think is that it probably takes as much, or more, courage to stand up for sexual liberation today than it did when I began.

First of all, in 1974, I had the protective cloak of a cultural convolution, the "sexual revolution," to wrap around myself.

Second, when I started out, there was not an AIDS epidemic.

Back then, the risks associated with sex itself were an unwanted pregnancy or a painful but not fatal STD. Not death.

We had the luxury of a certain innocence; we did not have to know the term safe sex.

There were no viperish fanatics out there preaching that an agonizing death from an incurable disease was the just wages of sin.

There had not yet been any mid-1980s swing of the pendulum wherein, in an honorable effort to expose the devastating statistics concerning sexual violence against women and do something to stop the statistics' hemorrhaging, sex itself was made into the culprit of the crime.

Finally, McCarthyism was behind us when I opened Eve's Garden. There was yet no Bush administration, neither King nor Princeling, and no appointees like John Ashcroft who were using the credibility and power of their positions to forward a constipated agenda or lead an active and dangerous anti-civil rights campaign.

What I really think is that Alice Paul, suffering forced feedings and beatings in a filthy jail cell to win American women the right to vote, had courage. Me? I'm a little brave, a little crazy, and I have a great deal of chutzpah.

Chapter Twenty-Three

A Dildo Story

Finding new products to add to the inventory carried by Eve's Garden has long been my favorite part of the job. I like discovering that new finger-sized vibrator and being among the first to offer it to consumers. I like reading the new how-to books, being always open to new techniques, ordering the books and opening the crates and stacking them on the shelves. I love the *smell* of a stack of new books! I like watching an episode of *Sex and the City* and getting on top of stocking the pearl panties I know my customers are going to be asking for on the coming (every pun absolutely intended) business day.

A long-time interest in natural healing is reflected in a new department of the store—"The Healing Garden"—and I am currently engrossed in trying out various healing tools and remedies to develop that department's inventory.

Sometimes I have to be talked into expanding a frame of reference before I feel comfortable about expanding into some new product line. For a long time, for example, I refused to stock any BDSM[14] gear in the store.

Sex, for me, had included issues of power in the past, and not in any positive or enjoyable sense at all. BDSM reflected, to me, an imbalance of power between partners in a sexual situation, and I found that off-putting, personally, as well as in conflict with my

---

[14] BDSM stands for bondage-discipline-sadomasochism.

feminist ideals.

My customers, however, were asking for handcuffs and spankers and such, and my sales staff, in turn, was asking me to reevaluate my position. Finding pleasure in submission—my sales staff asked me to consider—was not necessarily restricted to women being dominated by men. Plenty of men liked to be dominated too. Lots of strong women liked to lay it all down in the bedroom. Some *lesbians and gay men* liked to be dominated.

Still, I couldn't quite shake off my reservations about the whole concept of playing out power roles in an intimate situation in what I felt was an unhealthy way. Where was the potential for a heart-to-heart connection if it was restrained by leather? The *need* to dominate and/or submit smacked of patriarchal corruption, and it was, personally, more than merely unarousing. It was a turnoff.

I gave my staff what I thought was a final, emphatic, "no," and then it hit me. What was I doing *judging* the sexual preferences of those people who were into BDSM?

Come on, I asked myself, wasn't I spending the energies of my life promoting the position that sexual activity was a natural and joyous undertaking? Wasn't that position itself unacceptable to a sorry portion of the population? Didn't someone or other who didn't know any better judge me every day, and didn't I hate it?

Me, *judge?*

Far—far—be it. Not with a ten-foot pole, nor even a six-inch one.

There are now, of course, handcuffs and spankers and such on the shelves at Eve's Garden. The cuffs are the "soft" sort, and the spankers are pretty, heart-shaped things—I still can't bring myself to accommodate the heavy leather and steel stuff—but life, when one attempts to be fair about it, is compromise, and, when one is fortunate, it accommodates growth.

From time to time, I've been fortunate to add a product to the offerings at Eve's Garden that I've had a hand in helping to develop.

I'll tell you a dildo story.

One day, in the late 1970s, a man named Duncan Goznel came to see me at my shop. Duncan owned a company called Scorpio Products, in Brooklyn, and this company made dildos. Not just any kind of dildos—not the old, hard, plastic kind—but *silicone* dildos, which no one else was yet doing.

Duncan brought his new silicone dildos to my shop and gave me his pitch. Silicone dildos were pliable, and they retained body heat and therefore felt more realistic than the old-fashioned kind, and they were easy for their users to sterilize between different sexual partners and/or different sexual acts. All you had to do was pop them in the top rack of your dishwasher for a thorough cleaning.

Duncan told me his personal story. He'd used silicone in his work as an auto mechanic. When an accident left him paralyzed from the waist down, and he lost the use of his penis, he'd discovered what a great material good, old silicone really was. He'd created his pliable, warm, realistic silicone prototype so he would be able to continue to pleasure his wife.

I hadn't sold dildos at Eve's Garden prior to meeting Duncan. I did sell cylindrical vibrators, but the dildos that were on the market were all of such poor quality. Their manufacturers went to such great lengths to make them look like real penises that they just ended up looking deformed—a penis is a penis and plastic just won't cut it.

Silicone was a step up, but not perfect either.

Why did a dildo have to look like a cock at all, I asked Duncan? Did it have to have a well-defined, blushed-pink head, and blue veins in bas-relief? Maybe what a dildo was really all about was its shape—its ability to accommodate a woman's natural desire to be filled up.

My store manager at the time, Marcia Corbett, designed a survey that we sent to all the customers on our by-this-time-extensive mailing list. The survey posed this question to my customers: What do you want in a dildo?

The surveys came back: *shape*, my customers confirmed to me.

Something not necessarily large, but definitely tapered. Something not particularly wide, but undulated at its midsection. Something pliable and easy to care for. Something in a pretty color.

I spoke to Duncan and asked him if he'd like to try making a dildo following the suggestions of the women who'd responded to my survey.

Duncan readily agreed to the challenge and thus was the "Venus" born.

The Venus came, originally, in one size and two colors, pale pink and chocolate brown.

Now the Venus is widely available in three different widths and a variety of surprising colors. Duncan's company, now operating out of Chicago, still makes some of the best silicone dildos on the market though the competition from several woman-owned dildo manufacturers has filled my shelves with the fun and felicitous shapes of dolphins, whales, goats, and the Goddess, in every color of the rainbow.

Now I get to say that the customers of Eve's Garden were responsible for the fanciful and yet practical design of the dildo as we know and love it today.

Chapter Twenty-Four

Silence

More than thirty years after the fact, I was watching television and who came on the screen? The comedian, a big-deal celebrity, which is what he turned into after he date-raped me.

Every time I saw him on TV, I used to watch him with what I can describe only as a sort of morbid rapture—it made me sick to look at him but I couldn't take my eyes off of him.

I would get a choking sensation in my throat because I hadn't told about what he'd done to me, but I knew I couldn't tell now, not at this late date. What would be the use? The statute of limitations had run out long ago. All I would accomplish by talking now was to get myself crucified in the press for defaming a beloved and avuncular celebrity. I couldn't prove a thing—my word against his.

Still, he got to sit up there laughing with Johnny Carson while I got to sit in my living room and fantasize about kicking him in the balls and karate chopping him in the larynx.

Neither of my parents ever knew about Eve's Garden. My father died in 1966, before Eve's Garden existed, but I had my mother until 1978, and, still, I never told her about my business.

My brother and I spent an enormous amount of both physical and emotional energy making so many different arrangements for our mother's care in the last four years of her life. I moved into a bigger apartment, to a place up on Seventy-second Street, so she could come and live with me. I took her to stay for a while out on Fire Island. When, in 1977, we had to admit her to Payne Whitney for yet another flare-up of one of her many, minor physical issues—as well as her more urgent psychological problems—we were advised that the best environment for her would be one in which she could be provided with round-the-clock care.

Lorenz and I put our mother into a nursing home in Westchester County. Mom resisted this plan, and we felt awful about it. Going to a nursing home was not what Mom wanted; she just didn't care enough about living for either us, or herself, really, to hope that any other alternative was plausible. She wasn't particularly physically unwell, but she wasn't curious about anything. Lorenz and I would visit her frequently but she wouldn't engage with us, it seemed, no matter what topic we tried to talk with her about, or how we plied her with special treats or our own enthusiasms.

By the time I started Eve's Garden, my mother wasn't mentally well enough to hear about the store. She couldn't be confronted with her daughter's engagement in an activity with which she would have heartily disapproved: I was a proponent of masturbation, and I sold the tools that aided people in achieving masturbatory ecstasy!

I would have liked, however, to have been able to explain other facets of the women's liberation movement to my mother.

I would have liked to tell her that day care was now a political issue; that the courts were being pressured to crack down on deadbeat dads and make them pay up the child support they owed; that there was now a concept about equal pay for equal work—soon, maybe, women who worked as dress finishers would get paychecks of the same size as men who held those positions.

The one time I did attempt to have this conversation with my mother she was so distant that I didn't have the heart to keep talking.

Eventually, Mom fell and fractured her hip. Lorenz and I moved her to another nursing home, in the Bronx, to recuperate. She was confined to her bed there, supposedly just until she got well enough to walk again, but she really took to the invalid lifestyle. She lay in her bed and faded away.

She was gone from us long before she died.

It's my understanding that the comedian is now in a nursing home himself, and not well. He may even be dead before I finish writing this.

May he rest in peace. I've got bigger regrets about other things I never got to say.

Chapter Twenty-Five

An Orgasm a Day
Keeps the Doctor Away

When you're working on your eighth decade in the world, not only have you earned your place on the platform from which is dispensed advice on how to live a long and fruitful life, you're *asked* for your opinion.

Herewith, then, one of my gems: "An orgasm a day keeps the doctor away."

I said this even before I could prove it, when all I had to go on was the woman-wisdom that told me if something feels as good as sex feels, it has got to be good for you.

I had buttons bearing this slogan made up and I gave them away at Eve's Garden. I urged women, even if they were too timid to wear the buttons in public, to pin them on the headboards of their beds or on the sun visors in their cars to remind themselves of the benefits of the gift of sexual pleasure.

Now, of course, the myriad physical benefits of regular sexual activity are becoming well documented.

Sex, simply, is terrific cardiovascular exercise. You get your heart rate up, and your blood flowing; oxygen gets delivered more efficiently to your entire body. People who have an active sex life are less prone to suffer heart attacks.

Endorphins that are released during orgasm can dull chronic pain associated with migraines, arthritis, and other debilitating diseases.

Early studies show that frequent orgasm is linked to greater longevity, the prevention of certain cancers, a greatly decreased vulnerability to depression and suicide, and boosted efficacy of the body's immune system.

Want a good workout? Have an orgasm; a vigorous round of sex can burn up more calories than a whole boring spin class.

Want a great beauty treatment? Look in the mirror some time just after you've come—see that blush of healthy life on your cheeks? Who needs makeup?

Morning sex is not only an agreeable way to wake up, but the flush of blood through your system clarifies and focuses your thinking for the activity ahead; at night, sex relaxes the muscles, relieves the tensions and stresses of the day, and allows for peaceful sleep.

Sex is an all-purpose prescription—maybe not a cure-all, but grand preventative medicine!

And that little exercise routine you do specifically in order to keep your sexual muscles in shape—the Kegel exercises that strengthen your PC muscle and keep your pelvic sensations sharp? Regular practice of Kegel exercises[15] is the ultimate route to retain-

---

[15] You do do your Kegels, don't you? They're important for both women and men. If you haven't been doing them, start now; it's never too late. It's easy to identify the PC muscle: the next time you urinate, try to stop the flow in midstream. That muscle you're using to stop the flow is the PC muscle. Gentle but firm contraction, and then complete release of this muscle before the next contraction (release is as important as contraction), is the way to get it into shape; 10–15 repetitions per day are usually sufficient. For further information about Kegel exercises, *The G-Spot and Other Recent Discoveries About Human Sexuality*, by Dr. Alice Kahn Ladas, Dr. Beverly Whipple, and John D. Perry contains what is still the most comprehensive advice yet about how to do Kegel exercises. Incorporate them into your daily routine.

ing life-long urinary tract control. Do your Kegels and let June Allyson keep her diapers.

Sex is more than only a great physical workout, however; it is a spiritual meditation.

It's ironic that an activity that has been so condemned as a base animal instinct, mere bodily lust, a sin of the flesh, is actually the one human endeavor that can take us completely out of our body and connect us to a higher realm.

The rhythms of sex are a personal manifestation of the rhythms of the earth, the tides and the crest and crash of the ocean's waves, and a personal connection to those rhythms. Sex can transport us from the physical plane into our most creative and innocent selves at the same time that it reaffirms our union with the Mother, earth, who nourishes and sustains us.

Throughout recorded history, human beings have tried to locate God through prayer and meditation, hallucinogenic drugs or food deprivation, ecstatic dance, trance, and chant. They have punctured and prostrated, flagellated and even mutilated themselves.

Why is it so difficult to believe that we can find the divine through pleasure?

Or, maybe it isn't so difficult? Even conservative writers are growing aware of the potent connection between physical pleasure and metaphysical satisfaction. They are writing that married couples should pray before having sex and celebrate the most intimate marital act as a way to unite with each other and with God.

Though I know it would be a great miracle for a woman to achieve divine satisfaction through the androcentric model of sex approved by current conservative bias (and though I object strenuously to cosmic connection being restricted to only legally married heterosexual couples!), I am heartened that the intrinsic marriage of sex and spirit is at least—at last!—being openly acknowledged.

My exploration of Tantra and the techniques of conscious loving has led me to the knowledge that, for those who will cultivate the connection between sexuality and spirituality, sex is a form of worship.[16]

If you practice conscious sex with a partner, the bond that exists between you will deepen. But whether your rapture is solo or as part of a couple—whether the love you bring to the act is self-love or combined with tender feelings for others—sexual pleasure is a necessity for physical, mental, and spiritual well-being.

Regular orgasm is vital to a wholesome lifestyle—it enhances our health, our appearance, our self-esteem, our ability to function effectively, and our natural morality. Partake of it daily.

---

[16] For more on this subject, I refer you enthusiastically to both *Tantra: The Art of Conscious Loving,* by Caroline and Charles Muir, and *Sexual Energy Ecstasy,* by David and Ellen Ramsdale.

Chapter Twenty-Six

Adam's Corner

Besides enjoying sexual pleasure on a regular basis, a wholesome lifestyle also includes all those things we've always been told are so good for us and that seem to take such extraordinary human effort to maintain over a lifetime: a regular exercise routine, a nourishing diet, and avoidance of overindulgence in alcohol (and a complete avoidance of harder, harsher drugs). Smoking cigarettes is, of course, thoroughly discouraged to the point that partaking of the habit in public can, these days, make you feel like you're committing a crime.

I pass along my mantra of moderation, as well as the advice to approach the extraordinary effort of maintaining your health with pleasure (again, *pleasure*) in mind. Choose exercises you actually like to do, and choose whole, fresh foods to eat—these always taste so much better, and, no matter how your palate has been corrupted by fast and fatty foods, over time you'll start to feel so good, with so much more energy, that you'll develop a craving for them that will preclude any Big Mac attack.

I think it's good, too, to enhance your diet with nutritional supplements. Discussing with your doctor or other health care professional what supplements to take vis-à-vis your personal dietary needs should be a matter of course.

I consider myself lucky that alcohol has never been a personal demon, but I confess (just so you don't get the idea that I'm a saint) that I've been fighting with nicotine for most of my life, and I still backslide occasionally. That I've been known to enjoy a leisurely smoke after a meal is now my not-so-secret vice.

Other secrets to remaining vital?

Don't retire. I tried it once and it ushered in a period I look back on as an all-time low, a real depression. Or, if you do retire, don't do it with a jolt—one day you've got useful work in the world and the next you're sitting out in the pasture weaving daisy chains and going completely bonkers with boredom. You could say that now I'm *partially retired*; this can be, itself, a challenging state to achieve, but, for me, it's been worth the effort to balance an appetite for new adventure with (what has now become a real) appreciation for the rewards of past productivity.

Do stay current. Don't live in the past. Times change; adjust. *Be Here Now* is a philosophy beautifully expanded on by such writers as Eckart Tolle, Dr. Wayne Dyer, and Ram Dass, favorite authors of mine who all happen to be men.

Let's get down to the nitty-gritty of my take on *men* because I know someone, somewhere, is going to accuse me of male bashing in this book. I despair often that, for some people, an appreciation for women *is* the equivalent of male bashing. Why, oh, why isn't the phrase "equal rights under the law" simply self-explanatory? Let me say, for the record, it's not a competition. Women's liberation is not a matter of one sex asserting its superiority over the other—it shouldn't be and it can't be if we're going to fix the real underlying problem.

To undermine the fact that we're all of us in this together— whether the subterfuge comes from an old-time Lesbian Separatist or, more contemporarily, from Rush Limbaugh—it only makes the mess we're all in even more foul and puts off the day when our energies can be devoted to real healing.

Look, when I began Eve's Garden, men were banned from

entry. I've already explained that this ban had nothing to do with dislike for that sex in general—I personally think most men are pretty terrific; the ban had to do with creating a comfortable place for women to explore their own sexuality and, in 1974, this necessarily meant gender privacy.

Then, for a time, at certain specified hours, a man who was escorted by a woman was allowed inside my store.

In the mid-1990s, I opened Adam's Corner. For the first time, unchaperoned men were welcomed into the Garden at any time they chose to come. They even had a special section of the store where they could browse books and other products that were male gender-oriented.

That men are now welcomed into the Garden is a matter of staying current, of having changed with the times. I don't believe that the shame and guilt associated with the free and joyful celebration by a woman of her sexuality have been completely conquered, but enough of the battles have been won that she no longer needs to shop for a vibrator in a strictly sex-segregated atmosphere in order to feel comfortable—or even confident—in her role as consumer.

I think of this openness about matters of sexuality as one of the successes of the old "sexual revolution," as one of the fruits of the work I've been privileged to be a part of for over thirty years. When you can recognize some of your own contribution to positive cultural change, adapting to the change is especially sweet. You'll forgive me if I admit that Adam's Corner remains among what I believe are the most hopeful evolutions in the Garden.

Chapter Twenty-Seven

The Failure
of the
"Sexual Revolution"

It's not original to say that the media saturates us with images of sex. People have been both titillated by these images, and complaining about them for decades—steamy sex scenes on TV, models in their underwear in Times Square, scantily clad women and men selling everything from suntan lotion to motor oil.

There is nothing inherently wrong with these images, of course. I like looking at a fellow in his skivvies almost as much as I dislike the objectification of the human body in the cynical pursuit of profit—but that could be a whole chapter of its own!

What I really worry about is that we're presented with these sexually implicit images because they're supposed to be pleasurable to us. These visual pleasures, however, are heaped upon a people who haven't got a good, solid grip on how to be pleased.

For all the images that suggest hearty sexual appetites, we are a people who haven't learned how to feed ourselves.

Pleasure is not a natural ability in our culture and is no more a focus of our education than is the talent to drive a car. Yet we're expected to be able to pick up the skill as if it had been cultivated in us from birth, as if all of our lives we have been in training to adeptly fulfill the body's longings, as if, once we reach a certain age, or meet

a certain person, or participate in a certain legal ceremony—
BANG—the engine will turn over and off we'll go.

The clitoris, for example, is a thing still vastly misunderstood
by teenage girls—those scantily clad denizens of the local mall,
sashaying the food court as if they expect they know how to use
theirs to the best advantage.

It's like we're asking them to negotiate the Cross Bronx
Expressway when we haven't given them one single driving lesson.

Actually—sadly—it's not even that innocuous. It's like being
expected to manage the freeway while piloting a Ferrari going ninety
miles an hour and navigating around icy, hairpin turns. I mean, isn't
what we get from those media images the idea that everyone else is
having sleek, agile sex, so why can't we? And what's wrong with us
if we're not? What is AIDS to an uneducated person but the dead-
liest of hazards?

My Goddess, no wonder so many people choose to remain
behind the wheel of a ten-year-old Chevy Citation.

What was accomplished during the sexual revolution was
that we got increased *access* to sex—to sexual imagery, and sexual
opportunity, and birth control options.

Simple access, don't get me wrong, was progress; maybe even
a necessary first step, or a plateau. It is not a peak. If we stop where
we are, smug with this status quo, what we end up with, for all of
the access, is only *pressure*, pressure to have sex, and to have it often,
but not necessarily to have it well.

What was not accomplished by the so-called revolution was
increased *access to pleasure*.

Sex is still, in the main, based on the old, androcentric *bang
bang bang* model, and it is my prediction that it will remain so until
women, at last and this time with real feeling and tenacity, decide
that the model must be changed.

Women, I believe, will lead this next phase of the revolution because we are the ones with the most at stake. That men are, generally, at least physically satisfied by the conventional model of sexual pleasure is clear from the 5,000 years it has been in place (and, in many ways and in many lands, *enforced*). That women are less generally (and more sporadically) satisfied is clear from the testimony I hear every day.

Women will lead the coming revolution when we discover not just our very own clitoris—not just our trigger, the center pin, *the hot button*—but the magnificent, complex system of the clitoris.

The nerves of the clitoris extend from that marvelous little hot button like branches of the healthiest tree in a lush garden. They extend to encompass the vaginal walls and the uterus, to embrace the anus; they run along the inside of our legs to form a "saddle" of sensation, up our spines and into our brains, hardwired to our highest selves.

To foment this revolution, I'm going to recommend, and encourage, and insist, that you read Rebecca Chalker's lyrically written and fact-packed book, *The Clitoral Truth,* and let her take you on a tour of a woman's clitoris that is unforgettable, and life-changing.

And I'm going to recommend that you pick up a copy of Edward Eichel's video, *The Coital Alignment Technique* (CAT). This technique could rightly be called "the new missionary position." In this video, Ed uses both human models and animated diagrams to illustrate one of the most remarkable anatomy lessons of your life. With minor adjustments the old-style missionary position is revitalized to allow for greater stimulation of the divinely complex clitoral system. This both enhances a woman's potential for orgasm and continues to provide the face-to-face and heart-to-heart lovemaking that so many couples find so deeply connecting.

The bonus of this—men everywhere: listen up!—a man's

divinely complex sexual system is also stimulated to a greater extent by using the CAT. His capacity for lovemaking is extended, and his orgasms are more intense. Talk about more bang for your buck!

Writer Erica Jong puts it this way: "CAT promises an Edenic return to the kind of bliss that got Adam and Eve kicked out of the garden in the first place." Couldn't have said it better myself!

Victory in this revolution will not, you see, be one-sided. Men, too, have complex pleasure systems with yet untapped potential. A little knowledge, a little restraint, a little adjustment to the changing times . . . a chicken in every pot and a full-body orgasm in every bed.

The only thing we have to give up for a reward of this magnitude is 5,000 years of the fear of—and the attempt to control—the power of feminine sexual desire.

Chapter Twenty-Eight

Little Pink Pills

I sat down to watch the February 20, 2004 broadcast of ABC's *20/20* program with a glass of nice red wine, a few dark chocolates, and much anticipation. The show was titled *Women, Sex and Satisfaction*. Finally, I thought, some of the most prominent journalists in the business, on one of the most respected news shows of all time, giving the subject of female sexuality some serious consideration on a major network.

Boy, was I wrong.

The thrust of this show was not women, sex, or satisfaction—this was no fact-filled paean of awe to the beauty and intricacy of our clitoral network, and this was no tribute to the resilience and steadfastness of our Goddess-given sexual power through millennia of patriarchal repression.

The thrust of the show was to give credibility to a supposed medical condition, "FSD"—"Female Sexual Dysfunction."

Forget for a moment my initial confusion: FSD? Wasn't that that silly vaginal deodorant? The first question I have to ask the journalists of what is, generally, an accurate and reliable news show, is: what in the world were you thinking when you gave the program such a misleading title?

By calling the show *Women, Sex and Satisfaction,* the network raised the expectation that it was going to take a wholesome and holistic approach to the subject of women's sexuality. I was ready for a real education!

The show failed to do more than give some publicity to a condition that a lot of sexuality educators doubt even exists. Amid whatever research was managed for this show, did no one get wind of this doubt?

Moreover, would any network do a show titled *Men, Sex and Satisfaction* and then devote the lion's share of the segments to, say, premature ejaculation? Let me clarify even further: that would be a show about premature ejaculation; it would not be a wholesome and holistic approach to men's sexuality.

What there can be no doubt of is that the big pharmaceutical companies, and the men who run them, were well pleased with ABC's treatment of their disease. Talk about free advertising! The pharmaceutical companies are all, as I write right now, in a frenzied race to cash in on the windfall that will go to whichever one of them is the first to get to the market with that topical cream or the female Viagra tablet that can cure womankind of our natural sexual desire.

I fear that women—the too many of us who sincerely suffer from a lack of sexual desire—were left at the end of that television show with the conclusion that they are in some way defective, that they will sit in shame and silence, waiting for that little pink panacea to get FDA approval.

A woman's desire for sex ebbs and flows, waxes and wanes, over the course of a lifetime, a month, a day, much like a man's. With all due respect to Erica Jong, dedicated feminist, favorite author of mine, and coiner of the term "zipless fuck," women do not have all-weather cunts; what we have, unluckily and unlike a man, is the ability to fake it.

What we have, like a man, is pressure to perform and, exclusive to our sex, the ability to accommodate sex whether or not that sex is holistically satisfying to us.

The tragedy is that every time women force it and fake it, we perpetuate the myth of inherent pleasure in the androcentric model of sex.

Why in the world would women welcome a chemical "cure" that merely makes unsatisfactory sex less unappealing?

Instead of a pill or a cream to ignite artificial desire, I suggest another approach. How about a little foreplay in the form of relief from the stresses of modern life, a splendid meal in a quiet atmosphere, a long soak in scented bathwater, or a tender and intimate full body massage? How about a revival of courtship rituals in relationships, an environment of flowers, and music, and candles? How about setting aside some prime time for sex? (I have never understood why so many people leave the primarily important act of lovemaking as the last activity on their agendas, when they're already in bed for the night and too tired to do anything else!)

I suggest reading or viewing erotica together as a prelude to sex play; cuddling, to enhance mutual relaxation and affection; masturbation to climax prior to penetration to provide both ample arousal and a guarantee of satisfaction; exploration of techniques and positions and sex toys new to the partners to provide a sense of adventure and excitement in what might have become the exercise of routine duty; and consultation with a sex therapist—there are any number of very good ones out there; just be skeptical of their motive and/or credentials if the first thing they want to do is to offer you a chemical solution. (Find out which pharmaceutical company is giving them the bucks to procure guinea pigs.)

I suggest strongly that you read Dr. Linda Savage's brilliantly readable *Reclaiming Goddess Sexuality: The Power of the Feminine Way*. This book explains, in language that is both accessible and provocative, the nature of feminine desire. I can't imagine a woman who won't relate to Dr. Savage's analysis and be aided, in whatever stage she is in life, in her quest for sexual self-determination and celebration. I can't imagine a man who would go away from reading this book without an understanding so new and profound it would satisfy dear old Dr. Freud.

I have lots of other, niggling little problems with ABC's presentation of female sexuality as well. For instance, what was the purpose of that silly animated segment about what women really want, and why was it produced and narrated by a man? Why was the enterprise of two serious and well-educated young feminists dealt with so lewdly? The segment on CAKE, a New York- and London-based empowerment forum, could have been given more thoughtful treatment by a couple of snickering schoolboys than what the prominent journalists at ABC managed.

Here, then, is my challenge to *20/20*, or to any other news show that has the courage and wit and intelligence to take it on: produce a show that's really about women's sexuality. Hire Rebecca Chalker to write a segment on women's anatomy. It will be uplifting and educational for every man and woman fortunate enough to see it. Contract Riane Eisler to produce a segment on the history of female sexual repression and how that repression has deprived both sexes of the pleasure of our full sexual potential for far too many thousands of years. Get Marty Klein or Betty Dodson or Ruth Westheimer on board to talk about legitimate options for sexual therapy, and Charles and Caroline Muir to discuss conscious loving, and Gloria Steinem to provide her usual eloquent commentary about the role of the modern women's liberation movement in promoting healthy sexuality for both genders. Absolutely ask Rachel P. Maines to do a light piece on the history of the methods and mechanics used to relieve "female hysteria" through the ages—the piece will have to be light; her material is outrageous enough and we don't want rioting in the streets.

As for finding out what it is that women want, I can suggest a short list of a hundred or so people who'd be happy, I'm certain, to speak to the topic, and they'd be qualified to do it *because they're women.*

I'd even add my own two cents to that last segment: what women want is full social, economic, emotional, and sexual parity. Give us that and we're well on our way to putting all those scientists at the big pharmaceutical companies back to work finding a cure for breast cancer.

Chapter Twenty-Nine

Roe v. Wade

This chapter will be very short. I find it astonishing that, thirty-one years after the Supreme Court's decision to protect a woman's—and a man's—right to voluntary parenthood, the subject has to be addressed at all.

The year is 2004. The administration of Bush II is making headway in their attempt to revoke *Roe v. Wade*. The international gag rule, the ban on "partial birth abortions," the false rhetoric of the "culture of life"—they are chipping away at rights hard won by my generation of feminists. They are able to do this in a nation whose population is overwhelmingly in favor of choice because so many of us are sitting down and taking for granted our reproductive rights. The time to stand up is right now.

1. Educate yourself. Log onto *www.aclu.org* (American Civil Liberties Union) or *www.black-womenshealth.org* (Black Women's Health Imperative) or *www.feminist.org* (The Feminist Majority Foundation) or *www.msmagazine.com* (*Ms. Magazine*) or *www.naral.org* (NARAL Pro-Choice America) or *www.now.org* (The National Organization for Women) or *www.plannedparent-hood.com* (Planned Parenthood Federation of America) or *www.latinainstitute.org* (National Latina Institute for Reproductive Health). These

organizations have admirably done the job of doc-
umenting this debacle in the making, and their
Internet updates on the issue will be timelier than
anything I could possibly provide within a book.

2. Get outraged. Log onto www.prolife.com to keep
abreast of what the opposition is up to—including
the full text of Dubya's recent speech to the anti-
choice people praising them for the work they are
doing to take this basic right away from the
American people!

3. Write letters to your representatives and let them
know you are pro-choice. Let them know that you
are going to hold them responsible for their record
on this issue in every election in which they ever
run. Let them know that you know the facts: the
countries of the world in which women enjoy the
strongest freedoms are also the countries of the
world that enjoy the strongest economies. Put it to
'em that way. (Framing a pro-choice argument in
terms of the economy might even turn around a
few ideological die-hards, but I doubt it would
phase Dubya himself. Considering what he's done
with the surplus Bill Clinton left him, he clearly
doesn't give a fig about the economy.)

4. Send as much money as you can afford to the
groups who are fighting this attack on our rights.

5. Go march whenever and wherever these organizations are sponsoring a demonstration.

6. Register to vote and then actually get yourself to
the polls to cast your ballot—the anti-choice people
who are so efficient at mobilizing their minority

vote would be out of business if all of us mainstream people actually showed up at the polls.

That's all, except to acknowledge the gratitude I feel for all
of the women and men who helped to organize the "March for
Women's Lives" that took place on April 25, 2004 in Washington,
D.C. That the day was profoundly inspirational can be attested to by
any one of the 1.1+ million people who were there.

It was the largest protest ever staged in Washington.

I was there.

I marched and, I'll tell you what, at 82 I'm pretty damned
tired of having to go out and tread this same old ground all over
again.

Chapter Thirty

Flying

It's an odd experience, all of the culling of memory and the assigning of motivation that writing this book has demanded of me. I think I would not have been able to lead an unexamined life, even were that a desirable thing. I am much too curious by nature; the process of self-discovery has fascinated me as much as finding out about any other new thing.

I see, in the black ink on white paper that's becoming the story of my life, patterns emerging, and much that is contradictory. I see things I like and things that don't please me nearly so much. I like that I am a woman with strong opinions, and that I'm not afraid to give them voice, and I like my own fierce energy. I wish I had not lacked for mother-love as a little girl because the ever-after search for acceptance and confidence that has followed has hampered—at times, maybe, even crippled—the use to which I have been able to put my curiosity and my energy.

The lack of a firm base of unconditional love on which to build a life is, as I have already said, the great tragedy, sending the love-deprived to search for his or her base in unlikely, and sometimes dangerous, places—the solace of drugs and alcohol, the lashing out and revenge of violent crime, the resignation to defeat that leads to homelessness and madness.

That my own search didn't encompass such extremes of anti-social behavior I attribute to those things my mother did foster: an appreciation of the beauty in the world around me, and a need to surround myself with that beauty; an abhorrence of injustice and the need to do something to make my community a better place.

My search manifests in a quest for self-improvement, a desire to parent myself into the person I want to be. Participating in group workshops, as well as in more individual therapies, has enabled me, throughout my life, to bolster the sense of self-worth—and self-love—I've needed to accomplish the work that I have wanted to do.

In 1973, when I was still toying with the idea that would become Eve's Garden, my friend Jacqui Ceballos suggested that I take a course in EST training. She thought the theories on which the training was based would be a boon for me, and she encouraged me to go hear Werner Erhard at a talk he was scheduled to give in New York.

Werner Erhard spoke about some fundamental concepts of EST: the need for human beings to develop the capacity to live in the present; the necessity of recognizing that we don't always have to be right; the peace that comes with understanding that a thing may or may not work out, but we cannot ever know everything we need to know in order to move forward, and we can never know the outcome of the move. The bottom line is to be guided as we move by the investments our spirits are longing to make.

My spirit was longing to do something to facilitate women in the discovery and reclamation of our sexuality. Immediately after Werner Erhard's talk that night I signed up for a three-day EST training course. It was the final push I needed to move forward with my original concept for Eve's Garden.

By 1979, Eve's Garden's mail order business was thriving. It had been a year since my mother had died, and it was time to move on with my life, to the next project. I decided that I would expand Eve's Garden. I would open a street-level storefront.

There was some difficulty in finding a public place to plant the Garden. I looked at a lot of square footage, but when the landlords would find out that I was going to open a sexuality shop in their buildings, they would decline to rent to me.

Eventually, two gay men, who were partners in a building on Fifty-second Street, had the open-mindedness to take the risk of leasing to the owner of a sex toy store.

I called upon my brother, by this time a successful designer. He got to work gutting the existing interior of the building's ground floor and building a showroom for me. He hired a friend of his to panel the walls with natural, rustic wood, and to build bookshelves and display counters. Lorenz himself painted a trompe l'oeil of a garden in the store—flowers in pinks and mauves, and lush greenery; he made a charming little store for me.

From the day it opened, customers were drawn to my pretty shop.

They came not only because the shop was pretty, of course, but because it was a place where they could be comfortable in examining, discussing, and purchasing tools of pleasure. The excitement of each individual woman who entered my shop was palpable, and they all seemed to donate a bit of their intense energy to the shop before they left so the place seemed to become a container of collective, joyous discovery.

From a business standpoint, it was important that I offered my clients only the highest quality items, and it was important in terms of repeat business that I had a regular turnover of old inventory. There always had to be something new on the shelves.

I worked day and night myself, and somehow there was always money enough to pay for the staff I needed to help me keep the mail orders current while I expanded the retail portion of the business.

Still, the retail store was exhausting, and I was fifty-eight years old—almost sixty! It was disheartening to be struggling so financially.

When the offer came from an investor in Boston to plunk down a lot of capital, I eagerly took the meeting he requested. I suppose that the most important question I asked the investor was, Why do you want to invest in Eve's Garden? His simple reply was that he had four daughters. I understood that he was investing in Eve's Garden because he had a vested interest in being an active part of women's liberation and I responded to his offer with relief.

The investor hired an "expert" in marketing to come up with a plan to really rev up the business. The expert's scheme came down to closing the Garden's storefront and moving the mail order portion of the business to Boston. The fancy retail space demanded twice the effort of "mail order only" and returned not half the revenues. The shipping operation could be handled more cost efficiently from almost anywhere other than New York City.

So the expert said.

The changes the expert was proposing for the business, however, wouldn't be a step backward in the evolution of the Garden. The investor wanted to completely reinvent my mail order catalog, make it sleek and glossy, and he wanted to greatly increase the variety of items we offered in its pages. For one thing, he thought we should add a full line of sexy lingerie to our inventory—satin teddies and garter belts and string bikinis by Bob Mackie. He thought we should add fantasy masks, like the sort worn at fancy masquerade balls, all done with feathers and sequins and lorgnette handles.

My part in the reinvented Eve's Garden was to oversee the business's advertising and public relations—the tasks I enjoyed most and thought I was really best at, anyway. I could do this from New York. I kept my lease on the Garden's small, original space on Fifty-seventh Street to use as my office, and I rented myself a lovely loft in SoHo in which to live.

For a roommate I got a dog, a golden-haired, honest little

mutt I named Honey, and, for a while, I got some much-needed sleep and peace of mind.

After about a year, though, the problems that I sensed were being created in Boston started to feel critical to me, so I rented a car and packed up Honey and drove north to see what was going on.

When I got to Boston I found an entire echoing floor of an enormous warehouse stocked with merchandise and no one there shipping it out.

I found stacks of boxes containing another new printing of the new, glossy catalog and no money in the accounts to mail it out.

I found myself with a salvage job that I knew would end up taking me months to sort through.

The first thing I did was to draw Honey a bowl of water to refresh her after our long trip, and then I went to the post office and used all the cash left in the Eve's Garden bank account—a whopping $600—to buy stamps to get those new catalogs in the mail and the existing orders shipped out to customers.

Then I sat down to think.

The warehouse in Boston—the shipping operation that was to be so much less expensive when it was moved out of New York City—was costing a fortune. I decided that I needed to sell off most of the merchandise—all of that fancy lingerie and all of those feathery masks that my customers weren't buying anyway—and get back to basics: quality sex toys and the instructional books to go with them.

And I decided that I needed to get my business back to New York, where it had begun, and where I belonged, just as soon as I could.

I sublet my loft and took an apartment in Boston's North End where Honey and I would live while I sorted through the wreckage. I sold my house on Fire Island to finance the reinvestment I had to make in order to save my business. Eight months later I rented a truck, loaded it up with the merchandise that was left after my big sell-off, and started to drive home with Honey.

The truck broke down in Wooster, Massachusetts.

The only available replacement truck was so much smaller than that first one. By the time I got the inventory transferred into it, I couldn't see out of the back window to do any passing. I drove the whole way to New York from Wooster in the right hand lane.

Honey, who was a small dog with a correspondingly small bladder, needed to make frequent rest stops all along the way.

But Honey and I and our truckload of vibrators arrived in Manhattan in the early evening. There was time enough for me to unload the merchandise from the truck and into the small office on Fifty-seventh Street before dusk settled in.

We were home.

If ever I had need of bolstered confidence and uplifted spirits, I needed it while I was dealing with the fallout of the disastrous move to Boston. I signed up for another course of EST training, this time a six-day program.

One day of this training consisted of running an obstacle course, much like the ones that soldiers in the army are required to master, climbing down a straight cliff and crossing a ravine hanging upside down.

The last obstacle on these courses is always the hardest.

The last obstacle on the course at this EST seminar was a shallow but quite wide gorge that had to be crossed, from the top of one hill to the top of another. It was to be crossed via a rope. A bar was attached to the end of this rope and we trainees were supposed to grab hold of the bar and fly, like the trapeze people in a circus, across the gorge.

I had just turned sixty.

I stood at the top of the first hill, next to the instructor who was holding out the bar to me, and I wondered just how he expected a sixty-year-old person to be able to hang onto that bar all the way across that gorge.

"You know, you're an older woman," the instructor said. "You don't have to do this part if you think you can't."

"Son of a bitch," I said to the instructor, and grabbed hold of the bar.

And then I continued to stand there at the top of the first hill, wondering how my sixty-year-old hands were going to sustain the weight of my entire body for the duration of this trapeze ride.

"You're just going to have to keep on holding on," I told myself.

"Hold onto that bar," I thought, "the way you're holding onto your business, and don't let go."

Then I pushed myself off the top of that hill.

And I *flew*.

EST has now become Landmark Forum.[17] I continue to take training from them, whenever I need encouragement to engage in the process that expands my possibilities.

⁂

In 1982, after I'd gotten my business back from Boston (and myself across that gorge), I reopened my small, discreet, upper-office-floor retail space on Fifty-seventh Street, and Eve's Garden began, again, to prosper.

---

[17] Landmark Forum is located in all major cities, and many places in between. If you're interested in finding out more about their program, you can log onto *www.landmarkforum.com* for the location nearest to you.

Chapter Thirty-One

The Business
of Eve's Garden

The story of the business of Eve's Garden would never be suitable for use in a business school textbook. But, then, I didn't start Eve's Garden with the idea of accumulating great wealth; I started it as a way to do my bit for the women's movement.

The early 1970s were, in general, years of idealism fostered by, or left over from, the decade that preceded them. I was by no means alone in my willingness to step out on a limb for something I believed in. It was exactly, however, the purity of purpose with which I began Eve's Garden that resonated with my customers and allowed the business to evolve into a profitable enterprise. That I filled a need even I couldn't have known was so desperate, at a time when social conventions were shifting to favor ideals about which I was fervent, is almost beside the point.

My desire to promote whole and healthy sexuality has many times tipped the scale away from making a prudent business decision, and the business suffered for it.

I don't worry about the rent, but I don't take long vacations off pretty coasts in Europe either, and I stopped shopping regularly at Bergdorf's years ago.

That's all right with me, and I'll tell you why.

As I began to collect materials and memories to write this

book, I started to take a real accounting of what I've been able to accomplish in my life that might be interesting for someone else to read about.

What struck me was that, even with thirty years of owning my own business under my belt, I *couldn't* write a book for use in a business school classroom. I certainly hadn't stewarded my own interests as meticulously as I had my client list at Hodes Advertising. After thirty years of working my ass off (and I mean that; you should see my ass), I don't have a million-dollar baby to show off as the fruit of my business acumen.

I started to worry that, as the captain of a woman-owned, woman-oriented business, every success I came up short of would go against the tally of all the work that all women do for our families, ourselves, and each other. I started to have second thoughts about putting any of my story down for the record.

I began to wonder where so much of the money I did manage to make through Eve's Garden actually went.

Then my friend, Jacqui, reminded me how, one time, I put up the money to fund the first feminist speaker's bureau. It was only a few thousand dollars, but it provided the wherewithal to organize and advertise the availability of feminists to speak to women's issues on college campuses and with community groups across the country. Every dollar available was (and still is) invaluable to getting our message out there.

I must tell you how sweet it is to have an old friend who will remind you of things like that just exactly when you need them to. It made me feel so absolutely *rich*.

Chapter Thirty-Two

Has The Women's Movement Succeeded? Yes!

When was the last time you put away money in the bank toward your son's higher education but not your daughter's because, of course, she'd be getting married and wouldn't need to go to college?

When was the last time you saw job listings in the newspaper segregated by sex—"Jobs–Male: Board-certified surgeon to head up cardiothoracic unit" or "Jobs–Female: Must type 95 WPM, make brilliant coffee, dress herself attractively, be flattered when a male co-worker compliments her on the way her sweater defines her breasts, and understand that when we ask her about her marital status we are doing so only because we know that as soon as she gets her hooks into some guy she's going to leave our employ and start having babies."

When was the last time you cautioned a friend not to go out to look for interesting work in the world outside of her home because you feared she'd be emasculating her husband if she held a paying job?

When was the last time you used the phrase *loose woman* to describe a person who was enjoying a healthy sexual life?

Has the women's movement succeeded? Yes, without a doubt. A young woman is no longer expected, in this country, to go from the "protection" of her father's house directly into the "protection" of her husband's. A young woman who pursues achievement beyond that of making a home for a man and raising his children is no longer the exception. The ideals that my rebellious sisters and brothers and I talked about and organized for and struggled to attain in the 1960s and the 1970s have now been absorbed into the culture. We have created a new norm of freedom in our country.

The emergence of this norm is reflected in our popular culture. The shows we watch on television, and the ways that the women characters are presented, are a pedometer we can use to mark progress on the march through the past few decades.

Our first modern television heroine came to us in the early 1960s. She was Laura Petrie, played by Mary Tyler Moore on *The Dick Van Dyke Show*. Now, Laura was a contented suburban wife and mother who'd willingly given up her career as a dancer for one as a homemaker. But I say she was revolutionary, and not just because she didn't do the housework in full skirts and pearls but actually wore pants!

Laura and Rob Petrie were the first married couple on television who didn't have either an antagonistic relationship (like Lucy and Ricky) or an overtly paternalistic one (as presented on *Father Knows Best*). Laura and Rob really *liked* each other. You understood that their marriage was not based on a woman's need for economic protection and security—Laura was savvy enough to take care of herself! These two people *wanted* to be together; their mutual esteem was palpable and they functioned as effective and loving *partners*.

Next, still in the 1960s, came the single gals: Diahann Carroll as *Julia*, a nurse and a single mother raising her son, and Marlo Thomas as Ann Marie in *That Girl*, a young actress pursuing

226

her career on Broadway. Both Julia and Ann were very "moral" young women—I recall one episode of *That Girl* that was based on the premise that Ann and her boyfriend, Donald, finding themselves stranded on a car trip, had to share the only available hotel room. The comedy centered around a virgin and her man spending the night in a room that contained one bed. Both of these young women were also resourceful, whip smart, and economically self-sufficient. As Laura and Rob Petrie had provided role models for marriages of real partnership, Julia and Ann gave single young women their first popular models for independent living.

Let's return to Mary Tyler Moore, this time in the 1970s on her own show, *The Mary Tyler Moore Show*. Mary Richards embodied both the insecurities of the emerging female executive and the competence with which she performed her duties. She was abundantly respected by her male colleagues and trusted by her male superior. Also, she and her girlfriends (wacky as they all were) embraced each other in real friendship. While we never saw Mary's pullout sofa rumpled by anyone but our heroine herself, Mary Richards dated frequently, and we knew, thanks to one of the funniest innuendos I've still ever heard, that she was on the pill.

Mary Tyler Moore chopped out the path in the jungle and cleared the way for Julia Louis-Dreyfuss to be not just the female sidekick on *Seinfeld*, but one of the pals on an equal social and financial footing with her male friends and, integrally, on an equal sexual footing as well. Jerry and George and Kramer pursued the opposite sex enthusiastically, and so did Elaine. Jerry and George and Kramer got laid, and so did Elaine (when she felt her companion was "sponge-worthy," anyway). Jerry and George and Kramer failed as "masters of their domain," and so did Elaine—the star female character on the most popular television show in the country unabashedly masturbated; imagine how I cheered!

Finally, we came to *Sex and the City*. To call this show groundbreaking is being modest indeed. But presenting the normalcy of women enjoying sexual experimentation and sexual toys and, in general, joyfully fulfilling their voracious feminine sexual appetites, was not, I think, the point of the show. In spite of its title, the show was not so much about sex as it was about four sexually healthy, intelligent, and adventurous women who were *friends*. Carrie and Miranda, Charlotte and Samantha relied on each other. They supported each other through bad romantic breakups, championed each other's successful careers, eased the difficulties of childcare for new mother Miranda, and together nursed Samantha through breast cancer. The show set fashion trends and new standards for comedy excellence, and it was, certainly, revolutionary in its honest portrayal of women's sexual needs and desires, but it was a show that was really about sisterhood. The show's feminism is what endeared these four frankly New York women to women all over the world and is what, in my opinion, was truly groundbreaking about it.

Follow the evolution of popular culture for a quick walk through the evolution of how women are claiming our liberation. Many of the dreams of the women's rights activists of the 1960s and the 1970s are now mainstream realities.

I recommend a book to you that speaks directly to the point of just how values that were revolutionary only thirty years ago have become mainstream, and it does it in a way that all of us who are not social scientists can readily grasp. Now, I know that you may think I'm compiling quite a long reading list for you, but this book really does deserve to be at the top of it. It is one of the most exciting and important books I've read in a long, long time: it takes the results of meticulous research data and synthesizes them into a straightforward analysis of what the values of the American people really are as we enter this new century.

As a pro-choice, peace-loving Social Security recipient and beneficiary of Medicare, I would be alternately depressed and appalled if I had to believe that the values of the American people are represented by the Bush who was appointed to be the first president of the new millennium. This book I'm going to tell you about, however, inspires me with a great deal of hope: it turns out most Americans are pro-choice peace lovers too, and, if they are not (yet) personally affected by Social Security and/or Medicare, they do support the continuation of these two bedrocks of American social responsibility and compassion.

The book is called *The Cultural Creatives,* by Paul H. Ray, Ph.D., and Sherry Ruth Anderson, Ph.D. Dr. Ray is a graduate of Yale University, a former professor at the University of Michigan, and is now executive vice president of American LIVES, Inc., a market research and opinion-polling firm. Dr. Anderson is a psychologist and former head of the Clark Institute of Psychiatry. Drs. Ray and Anderson, a married couple, have combined their individual expertise in their own disciplines to create a landmark book that documents the fascinating story of the emergence of a new set of American values, and the people who live by them, and live *up to them.*

Drs. Ray and Anderson give a name, in fact, to what they call the emerging "subculture" of people who support the values they detail. They call us the "cultural creatives," and if you think the term *subculture* in any way indicates a "small" group of us, you're wrong—and you'd be as happily surprised as I was at being wrong!

But, before talking about the size of the group—and what the numbers mean to me—let's talk about a few more general ideas in the doctors' book.

First, I can't really define a cultural creative; I don't have the space in my own book to review the specifics Drs. Ray and Anderson address, and one really does have to go into specifics to understand the subculture (which is why you all need to go out and read the whole book yourselves!).

The authors, in fact, go out of their way to talk about how cultural creatives do not lend themselves so easily to definition—how we defy standard demographic categories. The authors do cite certain telling lifestyle choices of a cultural creative, though, and I'll list a few of them here: We buy more books and magazines, and listen to more radio, in particular NPR and classical music, than people in other subcultures. We are aggressive supporters of the arts and culture. We prefer quality to quantity and we are careful consumers (for example, we prefer a nice, heat-retaining silicone dildo over a cheap, plastic, poorly made one any day!). We tend to be trendsetters regarding knowledge-intensive products, including fine and whole foods, wines, and boutique beers (my enduring passion for Bud Light notwithstanding). Our homes are our nests, decorated for comfort rather than for fashion; our cars are safe and fuel efficient rather than flashy; and when we travel we shy away from package tours and cruises and prefer to appreciate exotic locations from an educational point of view, opening ourselves to the lifestyles and opinions of the native people as part of our learning experience.

The authors stress that cultural creatives will not do every single one of the things on this list of lifestyle choices and, as I've said, I've offered here only a portion of the choices the authors go into in so much detail, but if you found that you were nodding in recognition of yourself as you read some of the items in the above paragraph, you are probably a cultural creative.

Second, the authors explain how the subculture of cultural creatives was created: the civil rights and peace and women's liberation movements of the 1960s and the 1970s were explosive learning processes not only for the activists directly involved in those movements, but for all Americans. The good influence of these movements upon our culture has been to eradicate (or at least drive underground) the most overt of prerevolutionary sexism, racism, and ethnic prejudice from the mainstream.

Third, the authors talk about the culture wars as battles between "moderns" and "traditionals" over who gets to define America's social reality. The moderns are the mainstream in America—and have been from the country's inception. We are a nation of people oriented toward progress and mass consumption, bigger houses, better stereo equipment, and hotter cars, all made possible by a greater number of factories producing ever greater quantities of goods that provide ever greater numbers of zeros on dividend checks.

The traditionals are America's first counterculture. This group consists of people who moved away from the mainstream. Intimidated by or unable to cope with the pace of the modern world, they retreat into an imaginary America they believe was formed to remain static: a woman contentedly tending every hearth, a man at the head of every table, and every child learning to read from Scripture in a one-room schoolhouse.

The fight of the century wasn't between Dempsey and Tunney back in the 1920s—and it wasn't even that first contest between Muhammad Ali and Joe Frazier back in 1971; it is the moderns and the traditionals in ongoing combat for dominance over the interpretation of America's culture.

Now, however, there is a third culture in our country, the cultural creatives, and we are not so much fighting to interpret America's social reality as provoking good adaptations from the grassroots up.

All right, to the numbers now. They are rough and rounded in my presentation of them, but you'll get my point. In 1999, the population of the United States was about 193 million adults. Of these, 48% were moderns, 24.5% were traditionals, and 27.5% were cultural creatives.

The results of the authors' extensive survey show, in response to a question concerning profeminism in the workplace, that 55% of moderns were for equal rights for women, 45% of traditionals supported women's rights in a work environment, and 70% of cultural creatives were prowoman in the workplace.

You can do the math yourself, of course, but my extrapolation is that 110 million American adults, or 56% of the population, or a clear majority of Americans (however you want to put it), are more than no longer either fearful or contemptuous of the rights espoused by my generation of women's rights activists—they get feminism, and embody feminism in their everyday attitudes.

I'm sure a lot of those people still probably wouldn't call themselves feminists, but their attitudes, and importantly, their actions, speak more loudly than any label ever could. Of course, I'd find it refreshing if everybody could, once and for all, understand what a feminist is—simply: a person who recognizes that women are people too, and due all the same rights and responsibilities as male people—and accept themselves for what they are. But I'm willing to give them time to come to that place of acceptance (and, hell, I'm 82!) because the reality of this great expansion of the definition of people is already upon us. The numbers already speak for themselves.

Chapter Thirty-Three

. . . and No.

That last chapter was the good news.

Unfortunately, it's not all of the news.

Tell me, when do you think the last time was that the prom queen got raped by some football jock and didn't tell anyone about it because she was afraid some asshole would say she "wanted it"?

When do you think the last time was that a young woman got pregnant because she did not have access to appropriate birth control information? Or hid her pregnancy in growing fear and shame because she didn't have the wherewithal to drive across state lines for access to appropriate reproductive services? Or was forced to turn to some butcher to perform an abortion, and died from complications?

When do you think the last time was that some parent beat a child, or some creepy old man forced a young boy to whack him off, or some high school loser sold a fourth grader his first vial of crack?

When was the last time you understood in your heart that the tragedies of child abuse and pedophilia and the national epidemic of dangerous drug use among our young are all integral concerns of women's rights activists?

A society in which women, men, and children live together in safety, peace, and mutual support is the feminist ideal. You know that old saying, "If Mama ain't happy, ain't *nobody* happy"? Well, that's true. If Mama's not safe and sovereign, you think she's going to be able to protect her kids?

The comforting fact is that we live in a society where at least 56% of the population has integrated wholesome feminist ideals into our lives. When the sorts of abuses I cited at the beginning of this chapter do still occur, and we do learn about them, our hearts are open to the outrage the abuses should rightly provoke.

That's a start.

But getting comfortable is the first step toward becoming complacent, and right now, we need to be as vigilant as we ever have been. Right now, there are people in government office, or running for elected office, or "advising" our elected officials, who are very misguided in their clumsy attempts to create and sustain the sort of society in which the majority of us would like to live.

I am not talking only about the current presidential administration that seems to think that withdrawing federal funding from public schools won't harm our children, or that dismantling Social Security and Medicare as we know it won't consign a large percentage of our elderly to poverty, or that revoking the rights contained in *Roe v. Wade* won't do irreparable harm to our families.

I am convinced that the people who want to do these things—the people in the administration of Bush II and the state and local representatives who will continue to seek office long after this administration is gone in 2008—are not malicious, but are only acting in ignorance, *willful* ignorance, perhaps, I will grant you that, but the effort to educate them, and open their hearts, is still our ongoing task as long as any of them remain in office.

We must take this task very seriously. We must recognize that this will be a long-term chore, and that the consequences of failure on our part will be dire indeed.

We must also recognize that the problem of this sort of willful and stubborn ignorance will not be alleviated only with legislation, though that's certainly a big part of it. We have also to impress upon their hearts uplifting values. And there are some very basic ones that need to be impressed!

Did you know that in the waning years of the last century, in our own country, a small but influential group of religious leaders formalized their recommitment to the idea of the "biblically proven" inferiority of women? I was beside myself when I heard the news, although most people I talked to about it brushed it off as the prerogative of this small group to treat its women as they think the Bible directs them. They were willing to let this small group assume its own little bit of entitlement, its own little bit of contained female slavery, because it was contained, and so not going to have much of an impact on the rest of us. Of course, they thought such backwardness was pathetic but, in the end, would do *them* no harm.

My own feeling is that the brushing off of such ignorance is real elitist arrogance, with extremely harmful long-term and long-range possibilities, and I'll tell you why.

The Bible has been used to justify every sort of persecution that human beings have ever decided to commit. Early church fathers used it to burn women healers at the stake and to torture to death Jews who wouldn't abandon their own religion and convert. Plantation owners cited the Bible when they wanted to justify their ownership of African human beings. There are preachers in our day who quote passages from the Bible to support their defense of the thugs who brutally murdered Matthew Shepard.

Let's look at this small but influential group's recent claim from another angle. Suppose this small but influential group of religious leaders, a group generally believed to be benign and mainstream in their godliness, suddenly decided to restate their "biblically proven" superiority as white men over their fellow black citizens. The indignation and anger with which such a declaration would be met would absolutely set us on fire. No self-respecting American would consider such a group mainstream, or in any way benign. We would consider all of us to be harmed by such a shameful declaration and wouldn't want to associate with the group any more than we'd want to go to a Ku Klux Klan cocktail party or enroll at Bob Jones University.[18] A group that claims superiority of white over black should be, rightly, marginalized, and its policy makers shunned.

Why is it, then, that overt prejudice toward women in our society is met with only elitist disgust rather than the indignation and anger that would meet overt prejudice directed at any other group of people?

We are, as a nation, harmed by any group's claim of racial or ethnic or gender superiority because as long as one group of people is not assured of its sovereignty, then no group is. To claim the right to continue to subjugate women is no more a benign bit of backwoods cultural relativism in our country than female genital mutilation is in another. Whether a man believes a woman should docilely accept his authority by submitting to his words or to his knife, the conceit of a woman's inferiority is subversive thinking that endangers the welfare of over half the population of the world.

But, as I've said, the words of the Bible—the teaching of the gentle Christ—have a long history of being twisted by those who would themselves benefit by the manipulation.

Let me say, for the record, that living in a world devoted to the teachings of Jesus Christ would be paradise—He suffered the little children, for one thing; for another, He saved an adulterous woman from being stoned to death by cautioning the men who

---

[18] The fact that both President Bush II and Attorney General John Ashcroft have spoken recently at Bob Jones University does nothing to water down my point. I believe that the press has given the Bush II administration such a wide berth when it comes to tough reporting on controversial issues and accountability that most Americans aren't aware that the speeches took place, or they are unaware of just how racist the policies at Bob Jones University are and, so, don't know how horrified they should be.

would murder her that the one among them without sin must cast the first stone.

But read what some of Christ's "sinless" modern-day "followers" have to say.

Do you know who R. J. (Rousas John) Rushdoony was? He was an ideologue whose theories form the basis of Christian Reconstructionist (CR) philosophy. CR is a small but growing fundamentalist movement in the United States. Rushdoony wrote—it is the CR "Bible," if you will—a little text called *Institutes of Biblical Law,* and published it in 1973. This text offers readers the author's vision of an ideal world founded on Biblical law, based on his own explanation of the Ten Commandments and Biblical "case law" that derives from them. He details how this Biblical law would function in today's society.

The "Reverend" William O. Einwechter of Mercersburg, Pennsylvania, a Rushdoony adherent, citing Deuteronomy 21:18-21, writes that the penalty of death by stoning should be applied, today and in our own country, to adulterous women, homosexuals, and unruly teenagers: ". . . a grown son (and by extension to a daughter as well) who, for whatever reason, has rebelled against the authority of his parents and will not profit from any of their discipline nor obey their voice in any thing."

Einwechter continues, "The execution of the rebel in view is just, merciful, and preventative. Just, in that the transgressor deserves to die; merciful, in that his quick death prevents the destruction of the family, society, and others; preventative, in that it strikes fear in the heart of other would-be rebels and restrains them from taking a similarly ruinous course."[19]

R. J. Rushdoony died in 2001, but his son, Mark R.

---

[19] From Press Release, Americans United for Separation of Church and State, February 17, 1999.

Rushdoony, and other followers, like Einwechter, continue to spread his gruesome message.

Now, before you dismiss the Rushdoonys and Einwechters of this world as small-time crackpots whose views represent only the most dangerous and fanatic fringe of a mainstream and otherwise truly glorious religion, consider what Randall Terry, the founder of Operation Rescue, an anti-choice terrorist group and a close friend of the Catholic Archbishops of New York and Philadelphia, had to say to a group of his organization's volunteers (quote from the Fort Wayne, Indiana newspaper, *The News-Sentinel,* on August 16, 1993):

> I want you to just let a wave of intolerance wash over you.
> I want you to let a wave of hatred wash over you.
> Yes, hate is good . . . .
> Our goal is a Christian nation. We have a biblical duty,
> we are called by God to conquer this country."

"Hate is good . . . ."

I am an ordained interfaith minister. I've studied the teachings of the world's great spiritual leaders. I don't, however, believe that it takes years in a seminary to quickly see that sentiments like *"hate is good"* undermine—even discredit—the life and teachings of Jesus Christ.

Let me tell you about a very exciting and really satisfying experience I had recently.

I was out of town, visiting a friend, and she invited me to attend her worship service with her. I sat among the congregation of a small-town, mainstream Protestant denomination on a Communion

Sunday. The sermon that day was about Sophia, the woman who, in the Bible, represents wisdom. The lay minister—a man—spoke eloquently about the reverence the Bible directs us to bestow upon woman-wisdom. Then the church's minister—a woman—offered Communion. She broke the bread and spoke Jesus's words, "Do this in remembrance of me." Then she took the cup, raised it up, and spoke again, "Do this in remembrance of me."

This offering—these words—too many of us have heard spoken only by a man.

To hear the words of Christ, and the invitation to His Communion table, spoken by a woman is to feel wash over you a wave of inclusion, and peace. And love.

Yes, the women's rights movement has been a resounding success in many ways, and, no, we've got a long, long way to go before we can celebrate any sort of victory.

Chapter Thirty-Four

How Long?

Log onto www.cwluherstory.com, a Web site maintained by the Chicago Women's Liberation Union (CWLU). The CWLU was founded in 1969 by a small group of women. Veterans of freedom rides and peace marches and threats of terror from the Ku Klux Klan, these women brought their activist expertise to the cause of women's rights. On their Internet site, the CWLU provides an archive of classic feminist writing.

There is "The Myth of the Vaginal Orgasm," by Anne Koedt, written in 1970 and still, as cited by the Web site's editor, one of their most popular pages. There is "The Politics of Housework," by Pat Mainardi, also from 1970, "Why I Want A Wife," by Jody Syfers, and "The BITCH," by Jo Freeman, both from 1971.

The humor of these pieces is still biting, and revisiting the urgency movement thinkers felt about their topics in those early days is still thrilling, and inspirational. But I warn you, the laughter will end and the full flush of woman-pride the writing provides will slowly come to be accompanied by sadness: the things that women's rights activists were concerned about in 1970 and 1971 have not become antiquated worries. The writings are thirty-some years old, but the problems they address have not become quaint.

Sexual Politics, by Kate Millett, for example, though written in 1968, is particularly timely. In it she writes:

"One other device used to maintain the current and traditional sexual politics is to claim that the whole thing has already been settled a long time ago. 'We gave you the vote,' as the male authoritarian puts it with such stunning arrogance—we went to the polls and elected you into the human race because one day you mentioned the oversight of your exclusion and, obliging fellows that we are, we immediately rectified this very trivial detail.

"The foregoing is both a distortion of history and a denial of reality. Women fought hard and almost without hope, driven to massive and forceful protest which has served as a model both for the labor movement and the black movement. They struggled on against overwhelming odds of power and repression for over one hundred and fifty years to get this worthless rag known as the ballot. We got it last of all, black and white—women are the last citizens of the United States—and we had to work hardest of all to get it.

"And now we have it we realize how badly we were cheated . . . ."

". . . how badly we were cheated . . ."

And this written thirty-two years before pregnant chads!

I say it again: what is stunning to me is that more than thirty-two years after the Supreme Court guaranteed men and women our most basic reproductive right, we could still have ended up governed by an administration that would impose a global gag rule. This rule impedes any organization receiving federal funding from discussing birth control thoroughly with the people it serves, under threat of having its funding revoked. It shatters me that, thirty-two years later, there are still elected officials at every level of government who would reduce the quality of life, the sweetness of liberty, and the pursuit of happiness for men, women, and children worldwide.

How much longer will it be before we can take a breath, rest assured of such basic rights as *Roe v. Wade,* and move on to address other pressing issues of healing?

One other thing that Kate Millett does in her book *Sexual Politics* is to use the average year-round income of the white man, the black man, the white woman, and the black woman to illustrate the gender and race disparities of this measure of worth.

Well, what a great idea, I thought! I'll do a little current comparison, see how far we've come, and measure the success of women's lib vis-à-vis earning power.

Herewith:

	White Men	Black Men	White Women	Black Women
1968[20]	$7,870	$5,314	$4,580	$3,487
2001[21]	$39,834	$31,351	$29,930	$26,595

Here's a measure of success: in 1968, the difference between the income of the highest earners (white men) and the lowest earners (black women) was 56%. By the year 2001, that difference had shrunk to 34%. In 1968, white women earned 24% more than black women; in 2001 that percentage was 12.

Here's another measure: in 1968, women earned fifty-eight

---

[20] Ms. Millett used statistics from the Department of Labor; for purposes of consistency, mine come from the United States Census Bureau, which explains the discrepancy between her income numbers and mine that you will find when you read Sexual Politics yourself.
[21] Latest year in which statistics were available.

cents to every dollar earned by a man; by the year 2001, women's earnings had reached an "all time high" of seventy-seven cents to every dollar earned by a man.

Success? Some, sure. But I don't think a nineteen-cent raise in the course of over thirty years is any reason to cue the band and break out the bubbly.

Chapter Thirty-Five

Rev. Williams

Sexuality and spirituality—this is a topic I've talked about several times throughout this book, a link I've tried to make very clear, and I want to take one more opportunity to address it.

One of the longest walks I've taken in my life has been that between being a committed agnostic and becoming an ordained interfaith minister. I didn't begin my studies at the seminary until I was in my late seventies, so you can see what a long, slow walk it really was.

Frankly, when I was growing up, God offended me. I was born into a time when women were afforded few strong role models and a culture in which men were supposed to rise every day at dawn and give thanks to God for not having been born a woman. But that didn't mean I didn't crave spiritual succor.

My journey began when, as a young adult, I started on a search for what Karl Marx referred to as the spirit in a spiritless world. This longing for deeper meaning was sustained through extensive reading, most notably, of course, of the works of Wilhelm Reich. While I could understand and experience sex as a creative power, as being as one with the universe, and while I had a deep appreciation for the natural world, I did not revere the connection with the earth that sex provided. The connection felt, if you will, internal; sexual energy was personal power I was sending out into a (however glorious) void.

It was becoming involved in the women's movement, in the aspect of it that focused on our sexual liberation, that allowed me to take the next big step.

About the time that I decided to open Eve's Garden, I discovered a book called *Ancient Mirrors of Womanhood: A Treasury of Goddess and Heroine Lore from Around the World*, by Merlin Stone and Cynthia Stone. It was a compilation of strong, divine role models. The authors had spent three years in various libraries over two continents doing research to seek out the Goddesses of different cultures and to tell the stories about them that had been so long suppressed by the patriarchy. I thought that this book would be a thrilling read for women—it was certainly exciting to me to have evidence that my gender had once had entrée to the sacred without intervention by a male God or one of that male God's male earthly "representatives"—and I decided to distribute Merlin and Cynthia's book through Eve's Garden.

Then I met Merlin Stone herself. We had lunch together. She told me she had written another book—*When God Was a Woman*. This second book was supposed to have been just an introduction to *Ancient Mirrors of Womanhood*, but the material she'd found was so rich that the work had expanded to a book-length manuscript. The rich material that Merlin had found was overwhelming scientific evidence that the early Goddesses were, in fact, the world's first deities, worshipped by women and men the world over. No matter how remote these early civilizations were from each other, the myths they told of the divine Earth Mother had elements strikingly in common.

Reading *When God Was a Woman* was a revelation for me.

You see, like so many of us, my images of prehistory had been of a squat, square, cartoon caveman clubbing a woman over her head and dragging her by her long, ratted hair back to his cave.

I had believed that the male of the species had brutally dominated women throughout time. The few strong women who had managed to assert themselves throughout history were anomalies. I believed that we modern women were marching for a personal liberty that was unique to our era of evolution.

Discovering that, in fact, we modern women were not so much creating our power base as *reclaiming* it—as I had, indeed, put it: Eve *reclaiming* her Garden—made me feel mighty beyond words at my disposal to describe.

Merlin's book was but the first of many that would be written about the recovered history of our foremothers, the ancient matriarchies with their Goddesses and priestesses. But *When God Was a Woman* was the book that ground my politics. It also provided the epiphany I had so yearned for all of my adult life: it provided a divinity that was female and for whom *I* could be an earthly representative.

I began to really get it, why people had throughout time sought or revered a God or Goddess or Great Spirit. It was not a higher power that would dictate and oversee their lives that people quested for, but a loving connection with the divine, a oneness; a oneness that, as a woman, had eluded me through the putative and patriarchal God of my fathers.

Now I could look to the Goddess of my mothers:

In ancient caves of the Paleolithic era 30,000 years ago, the vulva was the first religious symbol, representing the doorway, our entry into life, our leave-taking at death. Our ancestors carved vulvas on cave walls, on rocks, over doorways and finally in temples. In India a whole religion exists around the symbols of the yoni [vulva] and the lingam [penis]. Indian theology conceptualized the entire universe as a manifestation of the activity of Shakti whose creative womb is incessantly active, continually spewing out all forms, all that lives and dies. This living womb, which is the creator of the universe and all forms, holds within her the mysteries of time and space. If you touch her yoni as you enter the temple, you will have good fortune in your life.

Women in ancient cultures were free in ways we can't imagine. Their sexuality was innately connected to their spirituality. How can this wholeness be understood by a people in whom the two are irrevocably split? We can begin to reclaim those earlier images and apply them to ourselves in hopes of coming into some form of contact with that original religious expression. We can begin to move in the direction of creating a world that includes a whole expression of sacred sexuality once more.[22]

I wanted to address the link between sexuality and spirituality following the chapters I wrote on the limited success of the women's movement because it is this link that provides me, as I hope it will you, with hope for the full integration of healthy, wholesome feminist principles into our daily worldview.

We are just beginning to emerge from thousands of years of neglecting our Mother. We are just beginning to heal the great wound where sex was torn away from spirit. We are doing it slowly, but it is happening. I see all around me new and renewed respect for

---

[22] Noble, Vicki, *Shakti Woman: Feeling Our Fire, Healing Our World: The New Female Shamanism*, Harper, San Francisco, 1991, a graceful and empowering book.

and connection to Mother Earth. I see, for example, reverence for the Great Mother manifesting itself in the widespread ecological and environmental movements. I see it in the publication of Al Gore's magnificent book *Earth in the Balance,* and in the Kyoto Protocol,[23] and I see reverence for our Mother in a humble blue recycling bin.

When I attended seminary, I studied the teachings of the world's great spiritual leaders and came to a stronger intellectual understanding of the natural link between sex and spirit.

I believe that when I finished my course and was ordained at St. John's Cathedral in 2001, I was the oldest new minister in the class.

My energies are limited these days—oh, the concessions one has to make to age!—but I'm delegating a portion of those energies to working with younger women and men who are dedicated to this healing message of reunion of sex and spirit, of the erotic as sacred. I continue to write informational (and, I hope, inspirational!) pieces that appear monthly on the Eve's Garden Web site. I am active in a group of interfaith ministers who meet in New York City on a regular basis to discuss the issues facing those who counsel spiritual seekers at the turn of this century. I sit on the board of advisors to a growing new organization, the Sexual-Spiritual Union Network.

To my readers, so that you will understand in an immediate and intimate way your own connection of sex and spirit, I ask you to remember that the next time you cry out, "Oh, God!" at the height of your sexual ecstasy, you are praying. You are intuitively recognizing that there is a connection with a force greater than ourselves and it is at this exquisite moment that you give up the ego and return to the arms of the Great Mother.

---

[23] Even though George W. Bush abandoned the Clinton administration's long commitment to this important international global warming accord with thirty other countries, refusing to sign on to it on behalf of the United States and further complicating our nation's already compromised standing in the international community.

Chapter Thirty-Six

Abundance

Abundance is defined as having more than a plentiful quantity of something; it is a fullness of spirit that overflows.

Abundance, to me, is having a towering, tilting stack of CDs next to my stereo. The stack necessarily includes Mozart, Beethoven, and Liszt. It necessarily includes Josh White, Placido Domingo, Sarah Vaughn, Mel Torme, Johnny Mathis, and Dinah Washington. It necessarily includes all four of my favorite different recordings of *La Boheme,* and my one favorite of *The Three Penny Opera.*

Abundance is having my bookshelves stocked with writers whose depth of insight into the human condition makes me close my eyes and sigh with satisfaction, no matter how many times I reread them: writers like Tolstoy and Dostoyevsky, Walt Whitman and Emily Dickinson, Arthur Miller and Tennessee Williams, Riane Eisler, Doris Lessing, and Tom Robbins. Abundance is my wide collection of feminist writings, books on spirituality and healing. (My vision is that one day I will go to an island in the Pacific with all of the books I have yet to read and dig in to them and fathom all that there is to know!)

Abundance is having membership cards to museums where I can go and lose myself for a day among works of art that were created by Marc Chagall and Georgia O'Keefe, Claude Monet and Frieda Kahlo.

It is reveling in having eclectic taste and appreciating so many beautiful things.

Abundance is good old friends, and new ones, an animal to live with you in your house, and loving the work you have to do in the world.

Abundance is a day at the beach.

Abundance is having the wherewithal—the time and maybe the money and always the heart—to help make the world a better place to live, especially for the children. It's organizing for better working conditions. It is happily paying the taxes that support public education. It is speaking out for women's rights because, in the end, it is a parent's decent job and a firm base of personal knowledge and a mother's dignity that impact most on how a child will be able to make her or his way in the world.

Abundance is doing away with labels. It is celebrating your own lifestyle, and the grand diversity of lifestyles that surround you, in peace. It is accepting all the fruits that nature provides with a grateful hand.

Or, abundance is—perhaps—one label, and that is *pansexual*.

Once, on a hike through a redwood grove, I stopped to rest by one of the big, ancient trees. I sat on the moss beneath the tree and touched its trunk. I let myself breathe in the moist, primeval air, and looked up into the dense canopy. I smelled the sweetness of the earth and the water and the moss. My senses were filled up, filled up with the necessity of making love to myself and so consecrating this sacred place.

Once, I was listening to a particularly beautiful piece of music while sitting in an open car on a balmy spring day and the soaring ascension of the notes so carried me away I felt an orgasmic wave pass through my body.

Once, on top of a cliff by the ocean in Hawaii, the waves were pounding the base of the cliff with such force that the force of the water came inside of me—that pulsing, rhythmic force—and I came.

Go, take your lover out under the stars and make love to her or to him; this is abundance.

Abundance is living in a society where, though women are still denigrated and our sexuality still exploited, every day I get to hear about, and even to meet, young people who are comfortable with being a little outrageous in good cause.

They are the students at Columbia University who I saw recently, strutting on the stage and absolutely singing the words to Eve Ensler's phenomenon of a play, *The Vagina Monologues.*

They are young women like Mama Gena who gifts the full force of her robust personality and natural woman-wisdom to the goal of helping women to heal and become whole.

They are Melinda Gallagher and Emily Kramer, founders of CAKE, who are carrying on the work of sexual liberation in important ways that are right for a new generation of feminists.

They are the 300,000+ young women and men under the age of 25 who marched with me in Washington, D.C. on April 25, 2004, all of them, from the stunning young women of the "Pink Bloque" who urged everyone to "shake your asses for equal access," to that gorgeous young man who so proudly led the chant, "Show me what a feminist looks like! This is what a feminist looks like!"

They are that little boy who I saw marching in Washington too—he couldn't have been more than six or seven years old. He carried a sign he'd clearly hand-lettered himself, bearing a sentiment I am certain he came up with on his own—"Don't be like Bush!" Putting aside the fact that I can too easily be moved to tears these days, that little boy made me cry with gladness for all of his potential.

They are all of the women of NOW, and The Feminist Majority, and all of the women's organizations the world over, including ones in India, Africa, and the Mid-East now struggling to stop wife-burning, genital mutilation, and other atrocities that continue in spite of the rulings against them in the United Nations.

Abundance is believing that a society that can make the arduous and heartbreaking trek from joyful and celebratory sex to sin can successfully make another journey, one that will bring them safely back home to the sacred.

It is having faith in the future. It is faith in all of the people on the ramparts fighting for a better world for all of us.

Chapter Thirty-Seven

Uppity Women Unite
(Emphasis on *Unite*)

Gratitude never radicalized anybody.
—Gloria Steinem

Abundance is picking up a book that you found inspiring in your youth and finding the concepts contained in it still valid.

Wilhelm Reich wrote, in *The Function of the Orgasm,* in 1940:

> Tradition becomes the bane of democracy when it denies the rising generation the possibility of choice, when it attempts to dictate what is to be regarded as "good" and what as "bad" under new conditions of life. Traditionalists easily and readily forget that they have lost the ability to decide what is not tradition. For instance, the improvement of the microscope was not brought about by destroying the first model: the improvement was achieved by preserving and developing the first model in keeping with a more advanced stage of human knowledge. A microscope of Pasteur's time does not enable the modern researcher to study viruses. Now suppose the Pasteur

microscope had the power and the impudence to prohibit the electron microscope.

The young would not feel any hostility toward tradition, would indeed have nothing but respect for it if, without jeopardizing themselves, they could say, "This we will take over from you because it is strong, honest, still relative to our times and capable of development. That, however, we cannot take over. It was useful and true for your time—it would be useless to us." These young people will have to be prepared to hear the same thing from their children.[24]

I become disheartened when I hear of bickering among generations of feminists. We let the mainstream snicker, once, while we divided and conquered ourselves. But there are still enough people who would force upon us compliance with outdated tradition without us doing it to each other. There are enough brambles and thorns trying to make their way into our garden without us nurturing rude plants in our own sunlight; we need every hand to the task of weeding.

To the generation now rising, I say: study herstory well, not so you'll be grateful for rights won in the past, but so you'll know where you've come from and won't have to repeat the mistakes of your foremothers. Take what we give you that is strong and honest, develop what is useful to your time, and go, go, go!

May the abundance of the Goddess be with you, and in you, at all times.

Blessings be.

---

[24] *The Function of the Orgasm,* Wilhelm Reich, Farrar, Straus and Giroux, 1973 reprint.

An Invitation,
and
Some Selected Writings

by Dell Williams

An Invitation

If you live in New York City, or if you are visiting the city and would like to stop by the Garden, our address is:

Eve's Garden

119 W. 57th Street

Suite 1201 (that's on the twelfth floor)

New York, NY 10019

We're open from 11 A.M. until 7 P.M. every day except Sunday, when we rest.

And, remember, no matter where you are in the world, you can always visit us online at www.evesgarden.com.

My papers are part of the permanent Human Sexuality Collection at Cornell University Library in Ithaca, New York. The citation is Dell Williams papers #7676, Division of Rare and Manuscript Collection. Brenda J. Marston is curator of the Human Sexuality Collection and its Women's Studies Selector. She invites researchers to consult the extensive description and guide on line at *http://rmc.library.cornell.edu/EAD/htmldocs/RMMO7676.html*. She also advises that there is lots of information to be found about the Human Sexuality Collection in general at *http://rmc.library.cornell.edu/HCS/*.

Many of the topics and concepts I have been passionate about in my life and, so, have explored throughout the years in my writing are, of course, contained within the text of this book. I have come across a few pieces, however, that address issues or points that bear repeating. I've updated them where it seemed appropriate and written brief introductions to them too.

Enjoy!

Female Sexuality: A Bill Of Rights

This short piece hangs on a corkboard over my desks both in my home and at Eve's Garden. It has hung in those places for over twenty-five years—the orange paper it is printed on is faded and the calligraphy and scroll artwork that adorn the words seem primitive in comparison to what any sixth grader can now accomplish with a desktop publisher. The words, alas, are not mine originally, but were composed by an anonymous group of women and passed on to me at about the same time that I started Eve's Garden. Because the words inspired me then, and because I still think they're right on target, I want to inspire you with them now.

We have the Right to:

- expect equal sexual enjoyment
- have our own orgasm——no pretending
- learn the true facts of the nature of our sexuality
- develop our own standards of sexual morality
- question the repressive aspects of religion as an inhibitive force
- enjoy both halves of the human race
- examine the factors that attract women to women
- withdraw from the sexual rat race
- explore our sexual potential through masturbation
- enhance our ability to fantasize
- preserve our sexuality and privacy if institutionalized
- demand respect for the sexuality of the handicapped and aged.

Nourishment from the Garden

I see education as my primary responsibility as the Gardenkeeper. I write an uncountable number of pamphlets and flyers about the nuts and bolts of such myriad topics as how to care for latex products and how to properly use a dental dam. I also write a great many similar pieces intended to encourage men and women to open their minds to sexual exploration. I see these pieces as education for the heart, nourishment for the soul. Three of my favorites follow.

The Whys, Why Nots, Whens, & Wherefores of the Vibrator

"Why?" a friend asked us the other day. "Why does anyone use a vibrator for that? What's wrong with bodies? Fingers? Mouths?"

You like Paris, we told her. Does that mean you shouldn't try London? Vibrators aren't a substitute for anything. They're another kind of pleasure. They can make you feel wonderful. That's why!

But some people don't like London. And some people don't like vibrators. They expect them to feel too mechanical. And that thought limits what they feel. So, if your head says no to vibrators, they may not do much for you. That's a good reason not to buy one—the only good why not.

When should you use a vibrator?

When you're alone, and don't want neediness to blur your judgment, or pull you down. (Sexual dependency can push you into bad relationships, ruin good ones, and make you think less of yourself. Sexual independence can add self-assurance to everything you do.)

When you're with your partner, to give pleasure to both of you. (With a little experimenting, it usually does.)

When you're in the mood for sex, or more sex, but your partner's not. (Obligatory lovemaking isn't fair, and it isn't fun.)

When you're tense and want a quick, easy way to relax. (But if tension has made you ache, begin by using your vibrator to massage away the knots.)

When you just want to do something that will make you feel like purring. (Isn't that reason enough?)

What Do Dildos Do?

There's a charming Chinese painting of three kimona'd ladies intently examining the wares of a traveling dildo salesman. There are dildos in museums, made of jade, ivory, silver, and wood covered in silk. They're found in the Kama Sutra and in the books and among the artifacts of almost every culture. Everyone knows where they go. The question is: What do they do?

Many women ask us. Here's what we know:

When you are sexually aroused, your vagina opens deep inside, like a balloon. You may feel a sense of emptiness, and a desire to have this space filled. When you don't have a male partner, that's something a dildo can do.

When your vagina begins that lovely, rhythmic pulsing, something inside can intensify that feeling. That's something else a dildo can do.

You don't feel that pulsing? Since the responsible muscle, the one that girdles the vagina, responds to both movement and pressure, a dildo may stimulate that feeling too.

And, of course, a dildo can also be used for anal penetration, even during heterosexual intercourse. That intensifies the pleasure for many women and, according to the most recent *Hite Report*, for most men.

But can a dildo, by itself, bring you to orgasm? Psychologically, yes, if it excites you enough. So can a kiss. Or a touch. Or a dream. Or a thought. But there's still a lot of controversy about the physical effects of penetration as the primary cause of orgasm. Orgasms can be felt in the vagina, but do they begin there? If so, what's a clitoris for?

Finally, we should add that we don't think of dildos as imitation penises. That's why ours don't look like penises. We designed them to be tactually and aesthetically pleasing.

They're sexual accessories. Not substitutes.

It All Begins in the Head

It's a shame that lust isn't more generally appreciated. Say the word and most Americans think of dirty jokes and dirty old men. So we were surprised as well as delighted to come upon these lines in a poem called *Two Songs* by Adrienne Rich.

I'd call it love if love
didn't take so many years
but lust too is a jewel[25]

These pages are dedicated to that sort of lust. The lust that is

---

[25] *Necessities of Life*, Adrienne Rich, Oxford University Press, 1976.

a jewel. The lust that is so full of joy it often grows into love. The lust that begins with, and adds to, self love.

Like love, that lust may be influenced by external things.

Being pleased with yourself helps. (Think of beautiful lingerie, a deep bed made with down and covered with crisp, pristine cotton.)

Fragrance helps. (Think of lavender, and honey.)

Touch helps. (Think of all the delicious ways you know to extend the language of touch.)

Technique can help. But not, we think, if it hurts your body or your spirit.

But external things are never enough. If they were, love and lust could be reduced to a recipe. Or an instruction manual. And all those self-styled great lovers who make such a big deal about technique might actually live up to their claims.

They don't, usually, because they don't ignite our minds. Only the mind can make the heart leap. And beat faster. Lust, like love, begins in the head.

But what the head can start it can also stop.

Think back. Did the wrong words ever stop you? Or an action that suddenly set your mind on the wrong track? Did you ever try to make love when you were angry? We are all so vulnerable when we make love.

Yet some of us are lucky. Because we're on good terms with ourselves, our sexual problems are momentary and few. We can play. Experiment. Ask for what we want. Like Voltaire, we realize that pleasure is the only rational human pursuit. So our lust doesn't make us feel guilty. It makes us more loving. And the pleasure it brings us buoys us up in everything we do.

If it could be like that for all of us there would be no more lying about orgasms. No more shame. No more going through the motions while mentally making up the laundry list. And every stale or exploitative relationship could be replaced with equality. And joy.

If that were to happen, we'd not only be happier, we'd also be healthier. And more confident. And more successful. According to a recent medical study on the effects of orgasm, we might even lead longer lives.

And it could happen! It does happen. Whenever we get the right information about our bodies and history and minds, and the right things to help us experiment, we begin to change our thinking. And that can change our lives.

There is no aphrodisiac as potent as thought.

Helping Your Patient to Help Herself

Eve's Garden produced this brief guide for physicians, therapists, and other professionals concerned with helping nonorgasmic women achieve greater sexual satisfaction. The guide was printed as a trifold brochure, and all through the 1970s I deluged doctors' offices and psychologists' offices and psychiatrists' offices and free clinic offices with it. I like to think that the lines of communication between health care professionals and patients are more open because of the women's movement: that women have been empowered to seek sexual health as part of good, overall physical and mental health, and that our health care providers are more able and willing these days to discuss women's sexual concerns.

I heard a jarring report, however, quite recently: in the current curriculum of most American medical schools, two hours of classroom time are required in the study of female sexual and reproductive health; seven to fifteen hours are required in the study of male impotency and the drug Viagra, specifically.

Perhaps tearing out or copying the following piece and then presenting it to your doctor is one of the ways you can voice your dissent about this gross inequity.

Although much attention has been given recently to women's sexual satisfaction, there are still many women who are not enjoying sex.

As a physician, therapist, or a person in one of the other helping professions, you have probably been asked for help by some of these women.

This booklet will help you deal with some of

their questions. It makes suggestions that you can adapt to your own professional situation, and to your own personal skills and training.

As a helping professional, you are a sex educator. You owe it to yourself and to your patients to be as skilled as possible, to understand their needs and to do what you can to help.

How you can help your patients who are not orgasmic or who are having other sexual problems

One of the most valuable ways you can help a woman to overcome sexual problems she is experiencing is to listen to her. You will find that many problems do not require extensive sex therapy; they may require the clearing up of misinformation or clarifying what may be unrealistic expectations. Giving the patient an opportunity to bring into the open problems which may have been bothering her for a long time, being supportive of her concerns and providing her with essential information she may be lacking can help free her of some of the fears and inhibitions which may have been impeding her response.

Being comfortable talking about sexuality and sexual problems is important for you and your patients. Once a level of trust is established, communication will become easier and more meaningful. You might say to her, "I know this is hard to talk about." When inhibitions are affecting a woman's response, it is often helpful to explain to her that everyone has something about which they are inhibited, that the degree and extent of these inhibitions vary from person to person, and that she should not chastise herself for these feelings. Very often, once the woman can confide her fears or inhibitions, and the reasons for them can be explained to her, they will begin to subside on their own.

Many women are troubled by the question, "Am I normal?" This may apply to anything from the size or location of their clitoris or the appearance of their genitals to the nature of their sexual response. It is important that women receive the assurance that "normal" includes a wide range of responses, a wide variety of genital formations, and that size and location of the clitoris vary from woman to woman.

In cases where there may be some physical basis for dysfunction, or if the woman would benefit from more information on the physical aspects of sexuality, it is recommended that she see a gynecologist who will examine her thoroughly, and who will take the time to answer her questions.

A brief program of sex therapy for the nonorgasmic woman

For the woman who has not experienced orgasm, or who experiences it infrequently, a brief program of self-help sex therapy offers an excellent prognosis. Lack of orgasm in women is the easiest of all sexual dysfunctions to cure. The therapeutic regimen can be undertaken by the woman herself, without involving her partner.

In fact, one of the most important aspects of the program is to encourage the woman to take some time each day for herself, by herself, away from the demands of her family, her job, and all of the other stresses she normally experiences. Even if it's just fifteen minutes a day, it is important that she take this time for herself.

Encourage her to explore her body and her sensuality, to learn what feels good to her. Reestablishing a person's inborn sensuality and trust in their own body is an essential step toward the building of a positive sexual self-image. The ability to relax and enjoy her body can help relieve some of the pressures of sexual performance which afflict many women.

It is important to allow her to move at her own pace, to talk about her reaction to these sensual experiences, and to bring out into the open any inhibitions she may feel about these experiences.

Once a sense of trust in her own sensuality is established, suggest that she include sexual touching as part of her self-exploration. Talk about masturbation with her. Explain that although inhibitions about masturbation exist, studies have shown that most people do masturbate. Masturbation is an excellent technique for learning what is pleasing and for achieving sexual fulfillment. Many women can reach orgasm through masturbation who are not orgasmic during intercourse. Encourage her to explore her genitals, to try different techniques of self-stimulation, so she can ascertain what is most pleasing to her. There should be no implied pressure about reaching orgasm. She should be focused on the process, not on the goal!

For many women, a vibrator is a helpful sexual aid. Once a woman has become comfortable touching herself sexually and has learned how her body responds to various touches, she may want to try using a vibrator.

Vibrators, which are available in a variety of designs, provide the intense stimulation many women find pleasing or more conducive to orgasm. Experience has show that 95-98% of women are able to achieve orgasm with a vibrator.

The next part of the process is to encourage the woman to share her masturbation experience with her partner, showing her partner what she has learned that pleases her, how she likes being touched. She may want to ask her partner to hold her while she masturbates, or she may want to show her partner what is most pleasing by guiding their hand. Once she is confident of her own sexual response, a woman should be encouraged to assert her needs with her partner, in a nondemanding, nonthreatening way. You might explain to her that many women do not reach orgasm from vaginal penetration alone, and encourage her to add whatever other stimulation she requires for satisfaction.

By providing a supportive setting for her to talk about her problems, and by encouraging her sexual self-exploration, you can enable your nonorgasmic women patients to realize the full joy of their sexuality, which will enhance their emotional and physical well being.

Sappho's Isle

For many years, in the early 1990s, I wrote a regular weekly column for Sappho's Isle, *a lesbian newspaper. The column was called "Sexually Speaking," and the four that follow address topics that are still current, and/or still touch my heart.*

"'Til Breath Do Us Part" addresses sex and aging. "To 'G' or Not to 'G'" focuses on the quest for our G spots. "The Best Sex I Ever Had" celebrates an early example of the sex-positive media exposure all human beings still so desperately need to be surrounded by. "The Language of Sex" is a reissuing of a 1990 invitation to you to help develop the sex-positive language our culture still lacks . . . and that I believe would go such a long way toward the healing we are all striving for.

'Til Breath Do Us Part

When I received a request to do a column on sex and aging, I stopped in my tracks. What did sex have to do with aging? Was it a problem? Does getting older affect our libido? And, what is getting older anyway except an archaic belief system! I'm 69 and I don't feel old—well, maybe I can't ski as fast as I used to, but I never feel old. Someone made that up.

The facts are that sex is as natural a function of the human body as eating, sleeping, and breathing. The Goddess granted us a body with the ability to respond sexually in many, many places. Our entire outer skin is one big erogenous zone, not to mention all the other places you are very familiar with. So, why would age affect our response? Again, it's all in the head. We create thoughts in our head, and these thoughts solidify into our belief system. So, if we think we are lacking in lust because of age, and since we manifest what we have been thinking about, we believe it. So, banish the thoughts!

My own experience has been that the "older" I get, the sexier I get. Perhaps that is because I have spent many years in an unfolding process of pulling away, leaf by leaf, the psychic wounds that bound me. Psychic wounds create fear and mistrust, the two elements that interfere most with the flow of intimacy, the flow of sex. When I was able to face my fear and break through mistrust, a space opened for love and lust to show up on a deeper level. And, who in our society has not been psychically wounded?

The only change that occurs with women through aging is the hormonal change after menopause that causes the thinning of the mucous membranes of the vaginal walls and a loss of elasticity. Try masturbation as a way of postponing the condition. It is also alleviated by the use of lubricants or by hormonal replacement therapy. To judge what solution is right for you, I suggest a consultation with your doctor.

So, you get my stand on sex and age. "'Til breath do us part" means until my dying breath. My friend Betty Dodson's vision is sitting in a rocking chair together with other women, and everyone is buzzing away with her vibrator.

Where there is life, there is the life force; where there is the life force, there is sex.

To 'G' or Not to 'G'

Whether 'tis nobler in the mind to suffer the slings and arrows of outrageous fortune and spend the rest of our lives caressing, celebrating, and adoring our clitoris, or to take arms against a sea of doubt and embrace the newly discovered but sometimes elusive and mysterious G Spot . . . that is the question!

And, so it has come to pass that after thousands of years of ignorance about the pleasure-function of the female anatomy, "The Jade Gate" is now open to ongoing scientific exploration. This may be the last frontier. We've already explored outer space without much benefit to humankind so perhaps we will explore inner space and do everybody a great service!

The New Age is exploring the vast potential of possibility that exists when one looks inward to connect with our very own consciousness, our very own heart, and our very own soul. We are coming home to where we belong, and that's really what self-love is all about. It is embracing our own humanity, vulnerability, woman-hood, and essence.

In 1982 the book *The G Spot,* by Alice Ladas, Beverly Whipple, and John D. Petty, was published, thus heralding in a new era of inner exploration by announcing that somewhere within the folds of our Jade Gate lies another source of erotic pleasure for women which they called the G Spot.

The G Spot was named by Dr. Ernest Grafenburg, a German obstetrician and gynecologist who, way back in 1944, first studied and noted the presence of this glandular tissue. Grafenburg, collaborating with a prominent American obstetrician and gynecologist, Robert L. Dickinson, who many regard as the first American sexologist, described a "zone of erogenous feeling that was located along the suburethral surface of the anterior vaginal wall."

A New View Of a Woman's Body, a book compiled by the Federation of Women's Health Centers (before the publication of *The G Spot*), noted that this structure of our anatomy was not mentioned in medical textbooks, and named it "the urethral sponge." They explained that it surrounds and protects the urethra by filling with blood during sexual excitement.

Perhaps the real credit for originating this study goes to

Helen Robinson, a feminist residing in Miami, Florida, who, curious about the erotic feeling she was experiencing from internal stimulation, did a lot of research to uncover the Grafenburg-Dickinson papers and was also instrumental in creating a study conducted at a women's clinic in Florida.

Unlike the clitoris,[26] which is mighty handy for our nimble and dexterous fingers, the G Spot cannot be easily reached because it is just beyond the reach of most fingers, although it is located only 2½ inches up the anterior wall, which places it about center in the vaginal canal. The authors of The G Spot advise that by sitting or squatting and applying firm upward pressure against the anterior wall and, at the same time, applying downward pressure with the hand on the outside of the abdomen just above the pubic bone, one might actually feel one's own.

The G Spot feels like a small bean resting in the vaginal wall but, when stimulated with pressure, swells to the size of a dime, or sometimes becomes as large as a half-dollar.

Other ways of exploring our G Spot besides fingers (your own or your lover's) are the G-Spotter attachments that fit onto the Hitachi Magic Wand or the Prelude 3. They are curved so as to be pointing in the direction of the G Spot and only about one inch in width.

I wish you happy, fruitful, pleasurable exploration!

The Best Sex I Ever Had

Several months ago, the headline of New York's feminist newspaper, *Womanews*, read, "The Best Sex I Ever Had." I thought, it's about time! I was elated to see this visible representation of grassroots sex-

---

[26] In this early writing I separated the G Spot from the tip of the clitoris; we now know that the places on our bodies that we identify as the G Spot and the tip of the clitoris are both part of entire clitoral body; I refer you again to Rebecca Chalker's book *The Clitoral Truth*.

ual liberation as front-page news. Whatever could be more liberating than women sharing their best sexual experiences? We share our problems and our pain; it's time to share our joy and our sexuality! Congratulations, dear Sisters at *Womanews* for taking a stand for the freedom of women's fullest sexual expression. I would suggest that these experiences be expanded into a book, and then into a movie! What could be more liberating than confronting a sex-negative world with the full power of our sexuality? It makes my head spin.

I think it is important for women's media to address issues around sexual expression, especially within a culture that still insists on keeping women subservient through sexual repression, as is clearly exemplified in today's fundamentalist and anti-choice movements. Their real targets are not souls or fetuses but women's sexual freedom and women's sexual expression.

Which is why I get really upset when I hear women who come up to Eve's Garden saying things like, "It took me ten years to have the courage to come up here," or, "My lover sent me for the dildo because she is too embarrassed to come up here," or "I always ordered by mail because I was too shy to come up although I live just around the block." I'm angry because that is exactly the way they want us to feel: guilty and shy and timid.

Well, I say it's time to be honest and upfront with each other about sex. It's time to share our best sexual experiences with the same comfort and ease we share our problems. It's time we greeted each other with, "Have you had a great orgasm today?" It's time we regard sex as a matter of health and really understand that having orgasms is a way of keeping us healthy and joyful and creative and happy, just as important as fresh air, exercise, taking vitamins, meditating, and eating a balanced diet.

We all need all of the affirmation we can get to continue to feel tall and proud about our sexuality. Orgasms are not only the most delightful experiences the Goddess created; they are also absolutely essential for good, radiant health.

Ancient Tantric texts used the words of SHAKTI to describe women's sexual energy. They understood it to be the creative force of the universe. Let us not think of it as anything less. Let us celebrate our creative force. Let us view it as our source of power, a power that regenerates and heals. And just let's forget all this stuff about being embarrassed and shy and timid about sex. It's the stuff of life.

The Language of Sex

If love makes the world go round, then sex is the motor. It is the generative force of nature that created all life on this planet. The cycle of birth, death, and rebirth is a manifestation of sex. But what is this powerful phenomenon that creates all life? What is the literal meaning of sex? I took a look at Webster's Dictionary to find out.

> Sex. The sum of peculiarities of structure and function that distinguish a male from a female organism; the character of being male or female, or of pertaining to the distinctive function of the male or female in reproduction.

How absolutely, positively boring, dull, and sexist. Yes, even the word sex is sexist because it assumes "sex" is only between man and woman. No hint here of even the vaguest description of the absolute delight of bodily and spiritual feeling that sex evokes. Only a matter of gender? Where is the language of sex that can describe the beauty and fun and wonder and joy of it? Even the words make love fall short of it. One doesn't "make love." Love is something you experience. Love is who you are. You don't "make" it.

The point is that we're all living in a culture that never, ever celebrated the joy of sex. As a matter of fact, it was exactly the reverse. Instead of celebrating the union of two bodies playing, dancing, caressing, touching, singing, hugging, loving . . . it was condemned as "Sin."

So, if sex is sinful and dirty, then there can be no language that is created to extol the beauty of it. That is why there are no words in our language to describe the act of physical love.

So, we really must start creating a new language to define one of the most treasured aspects of being human. The plant world created beautiful flowers, which are the sex organs of plant life, so surely we can do just as well if not better. Let us bring out the poetry, the music, the sweet sensation, the rippling splendor of the orgasm, and create a language to describe our experience, so that we can offer the future lovers of the world a language within which they can celebrate their sexual selves.

We call to the writers and poets and creators of words to redefine sex so that what has come to be known as *making love* is truly described to express the deep inner truth and spiritual ecstasy that is known today only by a word whose literal meaning is "gender."

If you accept my invitation, please send your responses to me via the Internet, at www.evesgarden.com. In my current monthly online column, "View from the Garden," I'll share with you the evolving new language.

The Eve's Garden
Pleasure Principle

The following pledge was included in one of Eve's Garden's earliest catalogs. It was designed to be clipped out, embellished with a bold signature, and posted in a prominent place to reaffirm the value and virtue of pleasure. I offer it to you in the hope that you will clip it out of its page in this book and use it to remind you on a daily basis of your own sovereign, blessed sexuality.

> Loving yourself is essential to a harmonious and balanced life. Touching yourself transcends the barriers that inhibit intimate physical communication with yourself. The act of self-love is taking responsibility for your own pleasure and leads to taking responsibility in other areas of your life. Self-love is your pleasure base. Your source of power. Your birthright. Your journey toward the ideal of learning to love others.

When you feel you have that right, you are ready to sign the Eve's Garden Pleasure Principle.

The Eve's Garden
Pleasure Principle

I pledge allegiance to the Eve's Garden Pleasure Principle. I agree to nurture, trust, and pleasure my mind and body to the fullest, secure in the knowledge that pleasure is my right and my responsibility.

Further, I assert my right to express my sexuality in whatever way, style, or situation feels good and loving to me.

I grant myself permission to be as bold or as gentle as I wish to be, both in reality and in fantasy.

In Celebration of Myself, and before the Goddess of Health and Pleasure, I hereby sign my name on this joyous day.

SIGNATURE_____

DATE _____

Essential Reading
and Other Resources

Many of the books listed below are referenced throughout this book. While they do not represent, certainly, all of the books that have been or are in current publication about sexuality, spirituality, and other women's issues, they are, in my opinion, the foundations. Eve's Garden is one source, of course, for the following materials.

Angier, Natalie, *Woman: An Intimate Geography*

Barbach, Lonnie, Ph.D., *For Yourself: The Fulfillment of Female Sexuality; For Each Other: Sharing Sexual Intimacy*

Barker, Tara, *The Women's Book of Orgasm: A Guide to the Ultimate Sexual Pleasure*

Blank, Joani, *Femalia*

Boston Women's Health Book Collective, *Our Bodies, Ourselves for the New Century*

Britton, Dr. Patti and Helen Hodges, *Complete Idiot's Guide to Sensual Massage*

Chalker, Rebecca, *The Clitoral Truth*

Cornog, Martha, *The Big Book of Masturbation: From Angst to Zeal*

Daly, Mary, *Beyond God the Father: Toward a Philosophy of Women's Liberation*

DeBeauvoir, Simone, *The Second Sex*

Dodson, Betty, *Sex for One; Orgasms for Two*

Eisler, Riane, *Sacred Pleasure; The Chalice and The Blade*

Ensler, Eve, *The Vagina Monologues*

Farrell, Warren, *The Liberated Man; The Myth of Male Power; Women Can't Hear What Men Don't Say: Destroying Myths, Creating Love*

Foley, Salie, Sally A. Koppe and Dennis P. Sugrue, *Sex Matters to Women: A Complete Guide to Taking Care of Your Sexual Self*

Haddon, Genia Pauli, *Uniting Sex, Self, and Spirit: Let the Body Be Your Guide to New Consciousness and Deeper Spirituality in a Changing Age*

Hite, Shere, *The Hite Report: A National Study of Female Sexuality*

Hutcherson, Hilda, *What Your Mother Never Told You About S-E-X*

Klein, Marty, Ph.D., *Beyond Orgasm: Dare to Be Honest About the Sex You Really Want; Ask Me Anything: Dr. Klein Answers the Sex Questions You'd Love to Ask; The Erotic Prism: New Perspectives on Sex, Love, and Desire; Let Me Count the Ways: Discovering Great Sex Without Intercourse*

Kuriansky, Judy, *The Complete Idiot's Guide to Tantric Sex*

Ladas, Dr. Alice Kahn, Dr. Beverly Whipple, and John D. Perry, *The G-Spot and Other Recent Discoveries About Human Sexuality*

Lightfoot-Klein, Hanny, *Prisoners of Ritual: An Odyssey into Female Genital Circumcision*

Mackenzie, Jordan, *Beloveds in Bed: 201 Secrets of Soulful Intimacy*

Maines, Rachel P., *The Technology of Orgasm*

Mariechild, Diane and Marcelina Martin, *Lesbian Sacred Sexuality*

Moore, Thomas, *The Soul of Sex: Cultivating Life as an Act of Love*

Muir, Charles and Caroline, *Tantra: The Art of Conscious Loving*

Muscio, Inga, *Cunt: A Declaration of Independence*

Noble, Vicki, *Shakti Woman: Feeling our Fire, Healing our World: The New Female Shamanism*

Ogden, Gina, *Women Who Love Sex: An Inquiry into the Expanding Spirit of Women's Erotic Experience*

Queen, Dr. Carol, *Real Live Nude Girl*

Ray, Paul H., and Anderson, Sherry Ruth, *The Cultural Creatives*

Ramsdale, David and Ellen, *Sexual Energy Ecstasy*

Reich, Dr. Wilhelm, *The Function of the Orgasm*

Savage, Linda, Ph.D., *Reclaiming Goddess Sexuality: The Power of the Feminine Way*

Silverberg, Cory, Miriam Kaufman and Fran Odette, *The Ultimate Guide to Sex and Disability: For All of Us Who Live with Disabilities, Chronic Pain and Illness*

Sjoo, Monica and Barbara Mor, *The Great Cosmic Mother*

Spong, John Shelby, *Born of a Woman: A Bishop Rethinks the Birth of Jesus; Living in Sin: A Bishop Rethinks Human Sexuality*

Stone, Merlin, *When God Was a Woman*

Stone, Merlin, Cynthia Stone, *Ancient Mirrors of Womanhood: A Treasury of Goddess and Heroine Lore from Around the World*

Tiefer, Leonore, *Sex Is Not a Natural Act & Other Essays*

Thomashauer, Regena, *Mama Gena's School of Womanly Arts: Using the Power of Pleasure to Have Your Way With the World; Mama Gena's Owner's and Operator's Guide to Men*

Wolfe, Janet, Ph.D., *What To Do When He Has A Headache*

Video

Eichel, Edward, *The Coital Alignment Technique* (CAT), www.marriagescience.com

Web Sites You'll Want to Visit

American Civil Liberties Union: *www.aclu.org*

Art of Being, The: *www.artofbeing.com*

Black Women's Health Imperative: *www.blackwomenshealth.org*

Body Electric School: *www.bodyelectric.org* (sacred sexuality)

Chicago Women's Liberation Union: *www.cwluhestoryww.com*

Cornell University Library, Human Sexuality Collection: *http://rmc.library.cornell.edu/HSC*

Dell Williams Papers: *http://rmc.library.cornell.edu/EAD/htmldocs/RMMO7676htm*

Emily's List: *www.emilyslist.org*

Eve's Garden: *www.evesgarden.com*

Feminist Majority Foundation, The: *www.feminist.org*

Harbin Hot Springs: *www.harbin.org* (healing and sacred sex retreats)

Institute for Ecstatic Living: *www.ecstaticliving.com* (sacred sexuality)

Klein, Dr. Marty: *www.newsletter@SexEd.org*

Landmark Forum: *www.landmarkforum.com* (self-improvement)

Move On: *www.moveon.org*

Ms. Magazine: *www.msmagazine.com*

NARAL Pro-Choice America: *www.naral.org*

National Latina Institute for Reproductive Health: *www.latinainstitute.org*

National Organization for Women, The: *www.now.org*

Planned Parenthood Federation of America: *www.plannedparenthood.com*

Ramsdale, David and Ellen: *www.sourcetantra.com* and *www.divinefeminine.com*

Shalom Mountain: *www.shalommountain.com* (healing and sacred sex retreats)

Veteran Feminists of America: *www.vfa.us*

Wild Hearts Ranch: *www.wildheartsranch.com* (artist's retreat/lesbian sacred sexuality)

Index

The Eve's Garden
Pleasure Principle

The Eve's Garden Pleasure Principle is as alive today as it was thirty years ago when it was written. Dell invites you to visit the Eve's Garden web site and receive a one time 10% discount at *www.evesgarden.com*. All you have to do to receive your discount is to enter the code on the bottom of the page with your order. Mention this offer and the code when you shop in person and receive the same discount.

If you would like to receive a 10% discount every time you order, just sign up to become an Eve's Garden Club Member. As a member you will not only receive a discount on all of your orders but you will receive great special offers and be eligible to win free prizes every month.

Over the years Dell has strived to make your visit to an Eve's Garden store or our web site *www.eves garden.com* more than just a shopping experience. Visit us today and take advantage of our special discount and enlighten yourself with the Eve's Garden Pleasure Principle.

CODE 1922